SELECTED TEACHINGS FROM THE
SELECTIONS FROM DIVREI YOEL
THE INTRODUCTION TO VAYOEL MOSHE
BY GRAND RABBI JOEL TEITELBAUM
Translated by Rabbi Joseph Kolakowski
Copyright 2007-2024

Contents

GENESIS/BEREISHIS 4
Parshas Bereishis 4
Parshas Noach 6
PARSHAS LECH LECHA 8
Parshas Vayera 15
Parshas Chayei Sarah 17
Parshas Toldos 20
Parshas VAYEITZEI 24
PARSHAS VAYISHLACH 26
Parshas Vayeshev 27
Parshas Miketz 29
Parshas Vayigash 31
Parshas Vayechi 33

EXODUS/SHMOS 36

- Parshas Shmos 36
- Parshas Vaera 37
- Parshas Bo 40
- Parshas Beshalach 43
- Parshas Yisro 46
- Parshas Mishpatim 48
- Parshas Terumah 50
- Parshas Tetzaveh 51
- PARSHAS KI SISA 53
- PARSHAS VAYAKHEL 55
- PARSHAS PEKUDEI 62

LEVITICUS/VAYIKRA 67
- PARSHAS VAYIKRA 67
- PARSHAS TZAV 79
- PARSHAS SHMINI 84
- PARSHAS SAZRIA 87
- PARSHAS METZORAH 90
- PARSHAS ACHAREI 91
- PARSHAS KEDOSHIM 93
- PARSHAS EMOR 94
- PARSHAS BEHAR 99
- PARSHAS BECHUKOSAI 100

NUMBERS/BEMIDBAR 102
- PARSHAS BEMIDBAR 102
- PARSHAS NASO 104
- PARSHAS BEHAALOSECHA 108

PARSHAS SHLACH	109
PARSHAS KORACH	111
PARSHAS CHUKAS	113
PARSHAS BALAK	116
PARSHAS PINCHAS	119
PARSHAS MATTOS	122
PARSHAS MASEI	123

DEUTERONOMY/DEVARIM 125

PARSHAS DEVARIM	125
PARSHAS VAES'CHANAN	128
PARSHAS EKEV	130
PARSHAS RE'EH	133
PARSHAS SHOFTIM	135
PARSHAS KI SEITZEI	137
PARSHAS KI SAVO	139
PARSHAS NITZAVIM	141
PARSHAS VAYELECH	143
PARSHAS HAAZINU	148
PARSHAS VEZOS HABRACHAH	160

SEFER VAYOEL MOSHE 162
INTRODUCTION	162

GENESIS/BEREISHIS

Parshas Bereishis

"In the beginning, God created..." (Genesis 1:1)

Rashi explains that the reason it does not say "the LORD created" is "because initially it arose in (God's) Thought to create it by the attributes of strict justice, and He saw that the world could not exist, so He preempted the attribute of mercy and partnered it with the attribute of strict justice."

This can be explained in light of the words of the Talmud that "Rabbi Eliezer taught that the world was created in the month of Tishrei and Rabbi Joshua taught that the world was created in the month of Nisan." Tosafos asks, "What did Rabbi Eleazar HaKalir base himself upon in composing the liturgy for the Prayer for Rain recited on the festival of Shemini Atzereth according to Rabbi Eliezer who said the world was created in Tishrei, while in his Prayer for Dew recited on Passover he follows Rabbi Joshua's view that the world was created during the month of Nisan? Rabbenu Tam answers that 'both this and that are the Words of the Living God'. The way to answer this is that it arose in God's Thought to create the world in Tishrei, and He did not actually create it until Nisan." Until here are the words of the Tosafos.

In a similar fashion, it is written in the name of the Arizal, to explain the words of the Liturgy of Rosh Hashanah "Today the world was conceived", that the term "conception" is related to the concept of "pregnancy", in the sense that the thought or "conception" precedes the act of creation or "birth". This is the meaning of "Today the world was conceived", that in Tishrei was only the thought to create the world, and it was not actually created until Nisan.

This is Rashi's intent when he writes that "at first it arose in (God's) Thought to create the world with the attribute of strict justice", meaning that initially the Thought was to create the world in Tishrei, which is the season of the strongest power of strict justice. Then He saw that the world could not exist this way, so He stood up and preempted the attributes of mercy, and created the world in Nisan, which is the month of mercy and kindness.

(Divrei Yoel)

Parshas Noach

"These are the offspring of Noah, Noah was a righteous man" (Genesis 6:9)

Rashi explains that this is to teach us that "the main offspring of righteous people are their good deeds".

In order to understand this, we must first understand the words of the Scripture, "also from the birds of the sky you should take seven by seven, in order to cause offspring to live upon the entire face of the earth". It would seem to be superfluous to say "in order to cause offspring to live", because it is obvious that is why Noah is bringing the animals onto the ark. However, Scripture seems to be saying that it was through the sacrifices that Noah offered after the Flood that he saved the world for the future, and God promised not to send another Great Flood. This is the intent of the Scripture, that from these animals (the clean kinds of which Noah brought seven by seven), Noah should bring sacrifices after the Flood, and in the merit of these Sacrifices it will be caused that "offspring will be caused to live upon the entire face of the earth", and that this was the reward for offering these sacrifices, that another Flood will not destroy the entire world.

This poses a question: It is known that there is no reward given in this world for fulfilling a mitzvah. However, the commentators write that when one adds to his obligation, going above and beyond the letter of the law, then there is reward even in this world. Now, Noah was not commanded by God to bring sacrifices. Since he was not commanded to do this, his reward for this act would come in this world.

The Bnei Yissaschar writes the following teaching to explain the term we see often used of "Mitzvos and good deeds". It would seem that they are the same thing. However, the term "Mitzvos" refers to those things we are obligated to do by the letter of the law, and "good deeds" are the things we add on our own in addition to the obligation.

This is how we can explain "these are the offspring of Noah", to which Rashi comments that "the main offspring of the righteous people are their good deeds". This is meant to refer to the sacrifices that Noah offered after the Flood, which are called "good deeds", since they were not commanded they cannot be called a commandment or "mitzvah". Through this, offspring remained from him, because as a reward for offering these sacrifices "offspring was caused to live".

(Divrei Yoel)

PARSHAS LECH LECHA

"And I will bless those who bless you" (Genesis 12:3)

There is a tradition that notes a connection between two Scriptures that say the words "And I will bless", One is here, and the other is "And I will bless Your Name for ever and ever". We may wish to explain this inasmuch as later in our Parshah it is written, "And Abram said to the King of Sodom, 'I lift my hands to the LORD'." The

Midrash Rabba notes that the Rabbis say that Abram sang a song of praise, as it says elsewhere "the God of my father, and I will exalt Him". It seems that we should explain this as follows: Abraham wanted to recite songs and praises to God because He saved him from the wars of these mighty kings. However, the holy book Noam Elimelech says on the verse "and he struck in on his inner thigh" that if there is a mixture of yetzer hara (an urge to sin) in a person's action, he is not able to use this to bless and praise God through song. If this is the case, Abraham was worried that if he took from the war spoils of these wicked people, he would not be able to sing a song to God, because maybe there was a mixture of evil into this deed. This is why he said "I lift my hands to the LORD", which the Rabbis explain as a song to God. This is why he said "if I take even a thread or a shoe-strap from anything of yours", meaning that since he would not take from the spoils of these wicked people; he would not lose out on the songs and the blessings to God. This is how we can explain the tradition that links our verse of "I will bless those who bless you" to "I will bless Your Name forever". It means that God promised Abraham that he would be the source of blessing to those who are blessed by God, and

from now on he would not need to benefit from the wicked people. Through this, he would be able to bless God with full and acceptable concentration, because there would not be any attachment to the evil side in his actions. This is the meaning of "I will bless those who bless you", and through this you will be worthy to "and I will bless Your Name forever", that through the fact that God's blessings come to the world through Abraham, Abraham would be able to bless God with pure and proper intentions.
(Divrei Yoel)

"Go for yourself" (Genesis 12:1)

We can explain this according to the commentary of the Or HaChayim HaKadosh on the verse "and the LORD said to Abram, after Lot separated from him, lift up your eyes and see the land..." This verse proves that God was sitting and waiting for Lot to separate from Abraham, so He could show him the Land. First God tells Abraham "tell him of the Land I will show you", but He did not show him the land until he was separated from this wicked Lot. According to this teaching, one could say that this is hinted to as well in the Scripture saying "Go for yourself", that the words "for yourself" can be understood "go by yourself", as the Sages say elsewhere, "to them" and not to heathens, "to them" and not to dogs. Here, too, does God hint that the perfect way to travel is when "for yourself" is "by yourself", without Lot attached to him. Then, immediately, the verse is fulfilled promising "to the Land I will show you", according to the words of the Or HaChayim, that God did not show him the Land the entire time Lot was in his group.

(Divrei Yoel)

"How will I know that I will inherit it?"

There are two explanations of this verse. One is that Abraham was asking God for a sign that he should know that he will inherit it. Another explanation is that he did not ask for a sign, but rather he said before God, "Lord of the world, let me know what merit I will have to fulfill it?" God answered him, "in the merit of the sacrificial offerings". Both explanations are difficult to understand. The first explanation that he was asking for a sign is certainly very difficult to imagine this, that Abraham did not believe God's promise and asked Him for a sign. And if it was so, what kind of sign is this for God to tell him to take sacrifices to be offered? How does this sign hint to the inheritance of the Land? The second explanation is also difficult to understand, because the term "how will I know" does not seem to indicate this explanation. Also, God's answer of the merit of the sacrifices needs to be explained, because why did he need to take three of all of the different types of sacrifices? Why did he even need to take one sin-offering for all of this? We answer it by saying that Abraham did not ask for a sign from God out of lack of faith, but rather asked that God should give him a sign so he would known when is the true time of our salvation, because it is possible to err in this, as we have discussed above. And this is the explanation of "how will I know that I will inherit it?", meaning how is it possible to know when it is permissible to take over the Land, that it is already time? God answered him "take a three-year old calf", meaning all of the different types of sin-offerings, even the sin-offering of an individual. This means that all of Israel will repent of all of their sins. This is like Maimonides teaches that when the Messiah comes, all of Israel will return to God, and they will bring all of the sacrifices. This is why God told Abraham to

"take for me a three-year old calf" etc. This teaches us that when all of the different types of sacrifices are brought, and all perform full repentance before God, then we will know that it is the true time of the complete salvation.
(Divrei Yoel 5715/1954)

"And concerning Ishmael, I listened to you... and I will give him to a great nation"

We can explain this in light of the fact that the holy books tell us that in the future Ishmael will humble under Isaac. This is because even back then he repented at the end of his days, as it is written, "and they buried him (Abraham), Isaac and Ishmael his sons", mentioning Isaac first because Ishmael humbled himself before him. So too, in the future, he will totally humble himself under Israel, and all of the power of Ishmael will be given to Israel. This is the meaning of "and I will give him to a great nation" (the literal meaning of this verse, usually translated "...to be a great nation"), as if to say that "I will give" Ishmael to Israel, who are called "a great nation". According to the words of the Noam Elimelech in Parshas Behaalosecha, we see that Abraham prayed before God, and said "If only Ishmael could live before You". It seems odd, for why would Abraham pray for him? Did he not see how much trouble and pain Israel would suffer from him throughout all of the generations? The explanation can be found in the Midrash Rabbah on our Parshah (44:21), "And it came to pass, that, when the sun went down, and there was thick darkness" (Genesis 15:17), that God showed Abraham four things, Gehinnom (Hell), the kingdoms (who would subjugate Israel in exile), the giving of the Torah, and the Holy Temple. (God told Abraham that the last two would save us from the first two, and since the Temple would be destroyed, did he want his children to suffer on earth or in Hell, until the Temple is rebuilt.) God asked Abraham, "Which do you want your children to fall into? Hell, or exile under the kingdoms?" He chose the kingdoms, meaning that we would suffer under the yoke of Exile to be exempt from the suffering of Hell. Therefore, Abraham had to pray for Ishmael to live, this way we would suffer by the yoke of Exile under his hand, and be exempt from the punishments of Hell, see there. This is also the explanation of the Scripture saying "And I will give him to a great nation", that "I will give" Ishmael to a great nation, by sustaining him for the purpose and

benefit of Israel, who are called "a great nation", in order that through him they will be exempt from the punishments of Hell.
(Divrei Yoel)

Parshas Vayera

"And he sat by the door of the tent in the heat of the day"

Rashi comments, "It is written and he sat, because he wanted to stand up (to show honor to God), and God told him to sit."

We can explain this according to the teaching of the Zohar Chadash, where it says "What is the meaning of 'and the LORD appeared unto him'? It is that God showed a vision to Abraham and told him 'this generation will be righteous, and this generation will be on an intermediate level of piety, and this generation will be wicked'." (Until here are the words of the Zohar Chadash.)

When our father Abraham saw the lowly situation of this final generation, he wanted to establish a power to save us, therefore he wanted to "stand up", as our Sages have taught that "standing" refers to prayer. It means that he wanted to pray prayers like those that would force the Redemption to come quicker, like we see with the prayers of Rabbi Chiya and his sons. However, even this prayer falls under the general oath that prohibits us from forcing the End Times to come, as Rashi explains that we are not allowed to pray over exceedingly for the Redemption. Some say that Rashi is referring to prayers like these that could force the Redemption like Rabbi Chiya and his sons. This is what is meant when Rashi says Abraham "wanted to stand up", meaning to pray for the final generations and to force the Redemption to come through the power of his prayers. This is why God told Abraham to "sit", and not to pray such powerful prayers, because this too is included in the oath that prohibits us from forcing the End Time to come.

(Divrei Yoel)

Parshas Chayei Sarah

"And Abraham came to eulogize Sarah"

Some explain this according to the law, mentioned in the Poskim, that in the days between Yom Kippur and Sukkos it is forbidden to say a eulogy. However, if it is at the actual funeral of a Sage, it is permitted to eulogize him. The Talmud says that the wife of a Chaver (Pious and trustworthy sage, a friend of the Torah) is like a Chaver. Therefore, Abraham needed to specifically go to his house to eulogize Sarah, because only in her actual presence was he permitted to eulogize her. This is because it is written in the "Asarah Maamaros" that the Akeidah (Sacrifice of Isaac) took place on Yom Kippur. According to this, Abraham came to his house close to Sukkos, as it was a three day journey to Hebron. This is why it says "and Abraham came to eulogize Sarah and to cry over her", mentioning his arrival close to the eulogy, because he was required to come to his house because of the eulogy.

(Divrei Yoel)

"I will go"

The Midrash teaches that in the merit that Rebecca said "I will go", Israel was worthy to the Exodus from Egypt. This is surprising. Some explain this that during the Covenant between the Parts, God said to Abraham "Your seed will be strangers in a land not their own for four hundred years". However, in the end they left Egypt after only 210 years of bondage. Rashi explains that the years of Exile were counted from the birth of Isaac, as all of the time the Patriarchs lived in the Land they were considered strangers. Now we should note the precise meaning of the verse where Abraham said "Do not take a wife for my son from the daughters of the Canaanites who I live in their midst." What difference did it make if he would marry someone from his own native homeland, inasmuch as they were also idolaters? However, in light of the above, we see that if Isaac would take a wife from the daughters of Aner, Eshkol, and Mamre, who were inhabitants of the Land, then their children would not be considered to be in Exile, because they would be citizens of the land from their mother's side. This is why our father Abraham said "do not take a wife... from the daughters of the Canaanites who I live in their midst.", because then the Exile would go further than four hundred years. This is why he said to take a wife from the daughters of his own family, who are not residents of the Land, therefore the four hundred years of Exile could be counted from the birth of Isaac. This is what the Midrash teaches that in the merit of Rebecca saying "I will go" were Israel worthy to the Exodus from Egypt. Because if she did not agree to go with Eliezer, then Abraham would need to take a wife for Isaac from the daughters of Mamre. Then the four hundred years of Exile would need to begin when they came to Egypt and not when Isaac was born. If that would have happened, they would have, God forbid, became so entrenched there that they would have fallen into the Fiftieth gate of impurity and would have never been able to leave Egypt. But, since Rebecca said "I will go", the four hundred years could begin with Isaac's birth, so they would not be so entrenched, and thus were they able to leave Egypt.

(Divrei Yoel)

Parshas Toldos

"And these are the offspring of Isaac son of Abraham, Abraham begot Isaac."

The question that the Commentators ask is well known, because what does the Scripture reveal to us here, saying that Abraham begot Isaac in the place where we are discussing the birth of Jacob and Esau? Would this not be more fitting in the place mentioning the actual time when Abraham begot Isaac? In order to answer this question, we must first examine the words of the Nezer HaKodesh on Parshas Toldos, who explains the words of the Sifri in Parshas Haazinu, where it is written "For the LORD is a portion of His people, Jacob the rope of His heritage". We see that from Abraham came the dross of Ishmael and the children of Keturah, and from Isaac came the dross of Esau and his tribal chiefs. But when Jacob came, no dross came from him; rather all of his sons were righteous like him. From where did God recognize His portion? From Jacob, as it is said "Jacob is the rope of His heritage". Just as a rope has three cords, so too was Jacob the third Patriarch. However, it would seem from the outside that the end of a thing has no connection to its beginning. However, the concept is explained that this is what the Scripture comes to teach us, that God chose the seed of Jacob at the Giving of the Torah more than the seed of Abraham and Isaac, because dross came from them and no dross came from Jacob. But this itself begs an explanation, because we need to know why was Jacob greater than Abraham and Isaac that he was worthy to have only righteous offspring and they were not worthy like him? This is why Scripture says "Jacob is the rope of His heritage", for just as a rope requires at least three strings, so too Jacob is the third Patriarch. As if to say that he was part of a "three-corded rope", and therefore his children were successful in their fulfillment of Torah and Mitzvos. This is as it says in the Talmud, in Tractate Bava Basra p. 88a, "Rabbi Yochanan says, anyone who is a Torah Sage, and his son is a Torah Sage, and his grandson is a Torah Sage, then the Torah will never cease from his progeny forever, as it says (Isaiah 59:21) "And for Me, this is My Covenant, says the LORD, for it will not leave your mouth, nor the mouth of your seed, nor the mouth of the seed of your seed, says the LORD, from now and forever more." What is the meaning "says the LORD"? It means that God Himself says "I will be a guarantor for you in this matter." And what is the meaning of "from now and forever more"? Rabbi Judah says, from now on the Torah will return to her host." (Until here are the words of the Nezer HaKodesh).

Therefore, we can explain the question of the Commentators, because the Scripture comes to let us know "and Isaac prayed to the LORD", and the Sages expound from this (Talmud Yevamos 64a) that "he was able through his prayers to remove the dregs and separate the attributes of strict justice. We did not find this aspect by Abraham. Therefore, the Scripture comes to let us know that he was worthy to this because he was the son of Abraham, and thus a righteous man the son of a righteous man. This is not like the scoffers of the generation, who said that Sarah became pregnant from Abimelech." This is why it says "These are the offspring of Isaac son of Abraham", that Jacob, whose progeny was perfect without dross, for Esau was not counted among the progeny of Isaac, as we said above. And how was he worthy to this? Because "Abraham begot Isaac", and he was a righteous man, the son of a righteous man. And then Jacob was a three corded rope, which does not quickly break.

(Divrei Yoel)

"And God should give to you from the dew of the heaven and from the fat of the land"

Rashi comments "He should give and go back and give again". We can explain that Isaac said to Esau "your dwelling place will be from the fat of the land". This needs to be explained. We can begin by explaining the difference between the peaceful rest of the righteous and the peaceful rest of the wicked. When it comes to the wicked, all of their peacefulness and joy is a joy that brings sorrow afterwards, may God save us. They begin with peaceful rest and end with suffering; for with all earthly pleasure, once the pleasure is finished one is only left with pain and regret. But with the righteous people who take delight in the LORD, after their joys come more joy upon joy. The holy books explain that this is the litmus to test any form of enjoyment and goodness, to see if it come from the side of Holiness and is pleasing to God. If more joy and goodness come after it, then it is from the side of holiness, and the opposite with the opposite form of pleasure, God forbid. This is the intent of the words "And God should give to you," that the blessing should come from God, meaning the side of Holiness, which will sprout more joy and goodness after this joy. This is why Rashi says "He should give, and go back and give again", to prove that it comes from the side of holiness. Therefore, he causes to have a giving after each giving, adding each time. This is not the case with Esau, by whom it says "your dwelling place will be from the fat of the land", and it does not say "and God should give", because his blessing was temporary, and at the end "his end will be eternal destruction" to Esau. (Divrei Yoel)

Parshas VAYEITZEI

"And Jacob said to Laban, give me my wife, for I have fulfilled my days"

It seems to me that this can be explained according to what is written in Chasam Sofer, for Maimonides writes "happy is the one who seals his days quickly", for each person has a measure of what he needs to fix in Torah and Mitzvos, and whoever completes this measure fulfills his purpose in life. However, if this person has children, then there is no set measure. This is why it is written "and the LORD will leave you over for goodness", that He will give you extra life for a good reason, "with the fruit of your womb", meaning that God will make your life longer so you can have a good influence on your children. Until here are the words of the Chasam Sofer.

This is why Jacob said "give me my wife, for I have fulfilled my days", meaning to say that "I have already finished all of the work I am responsible to fix, so I have already fulfilled the purpose for my life in this world." This is why Rashi explain that he wanted Laban to give him his wife in order to beget future generations, because then Heaven will give him more good life, only for the reason of begetting the Tribes of Israel. This is also what is written that Rachel told Jacob "give me children, and if not I am dead," because Rachel understood that she already fulfilled her life's purpose purpose in Torah and Mitzvos, therefore she asked to have children. Because, as we said, without children, it is as if she has no more years of life.

(Divrei Yoel)

PARSHAS VAYISHLACH

"I sojourned with Laban"

Rashi explains "And I observed the 613 commandments, and I did not learn from his evil ways" (The word "I sojourned" in Hebrew equals 613 in Gematria). We need to explain why did Jacob have to tell this to Esau? Perhaps we can explain this according to what is written in Tefillah LeMoshe (The Rebbe's ancestor, Rabbi Moshe Teitelbaum of Uhely's – author of Yismach Moshe commentary on Psalms) on the verse "And I am like a bountiful olive tree in the House of God." The Midrash mentions, "A beautiful form – the fruit of an olive – the LORD called your name". "Why are the Jewish people compared to an olive? Just as the olive only releases its oil through crushing, so too Israel…"

"Another explanation is just as oil floats on the top and does not mix with any liquid…"

"Every Jew has the choice whether he will be separate from the heathen nations of the world in all matters, then he will be called an olive that the LORD called his name, and will not need to be pressed. However, if he is not separate and tries to imitate them, then he will need to be pressed. This is what it means "I am like an olive", meaning that a Jew is compared to an olive inasmuch as he is satisfied to be rooted in the House of God, meaning he is separate and distinct from the heathen nations of the world; therefore he will not need to be oppressed." Until here are the words of the Tefilah LeMoshe

This is why Jacob sent the information to Esau that "I sojourned with Laban and observed the 613 commandments, and I did not learn from his evil deeds," therefore I am to be compared to the good oil that does not need oppression or suffering. This is because I separated myself from the wicked Laban, and therefore you do not need to hate me, because I do not need to be pressed. (Divrei Yoel)

Parshas Vayeshev

"And Judah said to his brothers, 'what will we gain if we kill our brother?'"

The Targum translates this "what money will be given to us if we kill our brother?" We can explain this according to the teaching of the *Tzafnas Paneach* who asks how the Israelites were permitted to take for themselves the spoils of Egypt, when they only asked to borrow these items. It would seem that they stole these items! The answer is that the source of the Egyptian silver was from what was brought from all of the other lands during the years of famine, when Joseph was distributing food and Joseph collected all of the silver and hid it for the needs of Israel. Therefore, they took what belonged to them, taking from what the righteous Joseph had prepared for them. It is explained that the promise of "and afterward they will leave with tremendous treasure" was fulfilled through Joseph's descent into Egypt. This is why Judah argued "what will we gain?" to say that if we kill Joseph it will not be possible for us to take the treasure from Egypt. Therefore, let us go and sell him to the Ishmaelites, and from there he will go to Egypt, and we will "go out from there with tremendous treasure".
(Divrei Yoel)

Parshas Miketz

"And Almighty God should give you mercy before the man"

The Midrash states "Rabbi Joshua ben Levi expounded this Scripture to refer to the Exiles, 'should give you mercy', as it says 'and he will give them to mercy', 'before the man', this refers to God, as it says 'the LORD is a Man of War'".

We can explain this according to what our Sages taught at the end of Tractate Sotah concerning the low spiritual level of the generation at the footsteps of the Messiah. They end their words saying "We have no one to rely upon except our Father in Heaven". It would seem that this is true in all generations, that we have no one to rely upon except our Father in Heaven, but it seems that in the earlier generations we had many to help purify us from the impurity of sin, namely the righteous people in every generation, who graced us with a spirit of purity and salvation. However, the Sages of the Mishnah bemoaned the situation of the final generation at the footsteps of the Messiah, for the righteous people are few and far between, and we lack the fulfillment from those people who can help us. Thus, we only have God Himself to help us and awaken a spirit of purity from Above. This is the meaning of "we have no one to rely upon except upon our Father in Heaven." This is the meaning of the words of the Midrash that says that Jacob prayed for the final Exile and for the future redemption, "And Almighty God should give you mercy", that God Himself will give us mercy and grace. This is because we have no one to awaken mercy upon us like in the previous exiles, such as when we had Mordecai and Esther, and the Hasmoneans, and the righteous people in every generation. In our generation, only God Himself will save us and redeem us!

(Divrei Yoel)

"And you will go up in peace to your father"

Rabbenu Bachaye writes that it could have said "you can go in peace on your way", however this is to hint to the Ten Holy Martyrs, who went up in peace to their Father in Heaven, after they were cleansed of the sin of selling Joseph. Until here are his words.

This seems difficult to understand. How could the difficult decree of the Ten Holy Martyrs be termed going in "peace"? We can answer this according to Rabbenu Bachaye's own writings, that he brings in the name of the Pirkei Heichalos, that Rabbi Chaninah ben Teradyon was traded with Lupinus Caeser, and it was Lupinus Caser who was burnt. In a similar manner were all of the Jewish Sages traded with Gentile Politicians, and it was they who were killed in their stead. Through this, they tasted a taste of death, inasmuch as they were arrested and sentenced to death, thus they received their punishment and it was as if they were killed. The Talmud says the term "you" specifies the people addressed and not their agents. This is what is hinted to by the words "'and you' will go up in peace to your Father", that you will be spared from the decree and go up in peace to your Father in Heaven, and not your agents, who will die in your place. (Divrei Yoel)

Parshas Vayigash

"And Israel said to Joseph, 'I can die this time, after I have seen your face, because you are still alive!'"

We can explain this by first mentioning the statement of our Sages that "A person should always pit the good urge against the evil urge. If he wins, it is good, and if not, he should study Torah. If that does not work, he should recite the Shma. If that does not work, he should remember the day of death." The Commentators ask, if remembering the day of death is sure to win, why does he not simply do so first? The answer is that remembering the day of death brings a person to depression and sadness. Thus, our father Jacob, who was suffering in his mourning over the apparent death of Joseph for many years, was unable to be worthy to have the Divine Presence rest upon him to prophesy. Thus, he was also not able to defeat the evil urge through Torah study or through recitation of the Shma, nor through the joy of performing a mitzvah. Therefore, he had to defeat it through remembering the day of death. This is hinted to in the statement of Scripture, "For I will go down to my son mourning to the grave", meaning that through the pain of mourning over Joseph, the Divine Presence was removed from him. Therefore, he said that he had to go down from his lofty spiritual level to defeat the evil urge by recalling the day of death. Now we can properly explain the statement of the Scripture, "And Israel said to Joseph, 'I will die this time'", because until now he had to constantly remember the day of death, and it was as if he were dying over and over again. But now he will only need to die one time, when the end of his life comes, and as long as he lives he will not need to remember the day of death. Rather he will be able to defeat the evil urge through the joy of fulfilling a mitzvah, through Torah study and recitation of the Shma. And the reason is because it is "after I have seen your face, for you are still alive", and I am able to serve the Creator through joy!

(Divrei Yoel)

Parshas Vayechi

"The angel who redeemed me from all evil, may he bless the children".

We will explain this by first understanding the words of the Nezer HaKodesh to explain the Midrash that teaches that "Abraham was only saved from the fiery furnace in the merit of Jacob." The Nezer HaKodesh explains that this is surprising, because it begs us to ask why Abraham was not worthy to be saved in his own merit, particularly considering that he offered his life to Sanctify God's Name. The answer is that really when someone offers his life as a martyr to Sanctify God's Name, it is better for him that God does not save his life, because it is one of the greatest forms of perfection that a soul can reach to die a martyr's death. This is why Abraham's life was not saved by his own merit, because it would have been better for him if he had been burned to death. Rather, his life was spared for the sake of continuing his holy and pure progeny, because he had not yet begotten an heir. And this is why the Midrash mentions Jacob as the one in whose merit Abraham was saved, because he was the first link in the chain that had only pious offspring. Really, the Midrash intends to say that Abraham's life was spared for the sake of the entire Jewish people. Until here is the teaching of the Nezer HaKodesh.

Similarly, we see that Jacob was persecuted by Laban and Esau, and he was saved from their evil only by tremendous miracles. It would have been better for himself if he were not rescued from them, because he would have enjoyed the tremendous level of perfection only attained by a martyr's death for the Sanctification of God's Name, because when one is killed by heathens simply for being a Jew one Sanctifies God's Name. The reason his life was saved was because of the progeny that was destined to come out from him. This is the meaning of "the angel who redeemed me from all evil", that God sent an angel to rescue Jacob in a miraculous fashion. Why did God do this? Because of the children, "to bless the children and call upon them my name," in order to establish future Jewish generations, following in the traditions we received from our Holy Ancestors. Without this, it would not have been worthwhile for his life to be saved.

(Divrei Yoel)

EXODUS/SHMOS

Parshas Shmos

"And he turned thus and thus, and saw there was not a man, and he smote the Egyptian."

The Midrash explains that when it says Moses "turned thus and thus", he looked into "thus will be thy progeny".

Some would say that the reason Moses slew the Egyptian was because the Talmud teaches that if a heathen smites a Jew it is a capital offense. However, this presents a problem, because there is an opinion that before the giving of the Torah the Israelites had the status of Noahides. That would present a problem, because if a gentile smites another gentile he is not liable to capital punishment. We must say that Moses was judging the case based on the future, because he knew that the Israelites were destined to receive the Torah, which would turn the case into one of a heathen smiting a Jew, which is a capital offense. The Midrash teaches that when God said to Abraham, "thus will be thy progeny", then was

Israel worthy to the giving of the Torah, as it is said "thus shall you say to the house of Jacob."

Now we can understand the Midrash that said "and he turned thus and thus" to mean that he looked into "thus shall be thy progeny", because from that verse was Israel worthy to the giving of the Torah. Therefore, they were judged as Jews even in Egypt because of their future status. This is why "he smote the Egyptian".
(Divrei Yoel)

Parshas Vaera

"And they did not listen to Moses because of shortness of breath and hard work. And Moses spoke before the LORD saying, 'If the Children of Israel will not listen to me, how will Pharaoh listen to me?'"

We will first explain this based on the teaching of the Midrash on the verse, "Why are Moses and Aaron disrupting the people from their work?" to which the Midrash says "you are 'why' and your words are 'why'."

I explained that the earlier sources ask "why we were redeemed from Egypt through Moses?" Didn't God promise "and also the nation that the will serve 'I' will judge", and it is written "and 'I' will also raise them up from them". The answer is that the promise that "I will judge" was only after the four hundred years of servitude was fulfilled. However, they only served 210 years, which is why the redemption came through Moses. (Until here are the teachings of the earlier sources).

In answering the question as to how the Israelites left Egypt before the time, the commentators answer that the difficulties of the suffering in Egypt made up for the time they did not serve. This would seem to contradict the above quoted answer to the difficulty of the promise of "I will also take them up from there" and "I will judge" inasmuch as they already served their time through the extra suffering of their bondage.

We must then say that this was Pharaoh's complaint against them, saying that the redemption was supposed to come through God Himself. He said that since Moses and Aaron were coming to ask the slaves to be freed before the proper time, he was not liable to free them.

This must also have been the reason why the Israelites did not listen to Moses, because they saw that the difficulties of the bondage in Egypt was indeed enough to shorten the time of their servitude, but their desire was that God would fulfill His promise to redeem Israel by Himself, when He said "I will raise them up", and take them out from Egypt Himself and not through Moses. This is why it says specifically that they did not listen "to Moses", because they did not expect God to send an agent to redeem them. And the reason was for "shortness of breath and hard work", because they expected that their shortness of breath and hard work would fulfill the time they had to pay, thus they did not want to listen to Moses, specifically to Moses. Moses then spoke to God saying, "If the Children of Israel will not listen to me..." specifically "to me", because of the difficulties we mentioned above. Therefore, he asked "how will Pharaoh listen to me?", to take them out from Egypt before their time, because if the redemption was coming through a messenger, this shows that their time was not fulfilled yet to leave Egypt.
(Divrei Yoel)

Parshas Bo

"Come to Pharaoh for I have hardened his heart"

We can explain this according to the words of my holy ancestor of blessed memory in "Yismach Moshe" to explain the scripture "And the sun rose and the sun came". We see that the reason the sunset is called "coming" according to the words of our Sages is because the sun sets in the west, and the Shechinah (the Divine Presence of God) is in the west, so that is the main desire of the sun is to be close to God. This is the meaning of "the sun rose and the sun came", this is the reason that sunset is called "coming" is because it says in Scripture "and to its place it desires to return", meaning to the place of God, thus it is called "coming back". Until here are his words.

Pharaoh was the source of impurity, and he angered God by saying "Who is the LORD that I should listen to His voice?". If so, it would seem impossible to refer to going to meet Pharaoh as "coming", because "coming" refers to coming close to the Shechinah, and by Pharaoh it was quite the opposite. However, since it was God who hardened Pharaoh's heart, and the reason for this was to fulfill the Will of God, inasmuch as his insistence not to send the people free was in order to show the Glory of God through him (i.e., that greater miracles would be shown through Pharaoh's insubordination to God), therefore it is possible to refer to going to see Pharaoh as "coming close to God", which is why it says "come to Pharaoh", the reason being is specifically "because I have heart".

(Divrei Yoel)

"And also a mixed multitude went up with them"

The Midrash Mechilta explains on these words that this is what God said to our father Abraham, "and after this you will go out with abundant treasure."

It seems that we can explain this according to Rashi's commentary on the Talmud in Kesubos, where he teaches that "someone who wishes to keep his possessions should always be giving them to charity, because by giving them away one will keep them."

Now, God promised Abraham "and afterwards you will go out with abundant treasure", which would mean that no Israelite would need to receive charity. This presents a problem, because that means that there was no one to give charity to. According to the treasure would not be able to be kept by them without the merit of giving charity. If this is the case, how can God's promise of them going out from Egypt with tremendous treasure truly be fulfilled, if they had no means to keeping it? This might be why God put it into the hearts of many of the Egyptians to convert to Judaism. Then the Israelites would be able to keep their treasures by giving charity to these converts, because they were not included in the promise of "leaving with abundant treasure", because they were not included in the decree of "and they shall serve them and be subjugated by them". This is the meaning of the Sifri that expounded the verse "and also a mixed multitude went up with them", that some of the Egyptians converted, and this is what the Scripture says that God said to Abraham "and afterward they will go out with abundant treasure," because through giving charity to the Mixed Multitude, the Israelites would be able to maintain their treasure. And, we see from here, that by the "blessing of

the LORD do you become wealthy, and you will not add sadness with it", that you shall not lose the treasure.
(Divrei Yoel)

Parshas Beshalach

"And it came to pass when Pharaoh sent the people out"

One may wish to explain this according to the well-known reason for Jewish exile being so that the Children of Israel should be scattered out across the entire world and bring out the holy sparks that were scattered during Adam's original sin. The Ohr HaChaim HaKadosh asks, (if this is the reason for our exile, and the exile is caused by our sins,) then if the Israelites have never sinned, and Israel would have never been exiled from their Land, then who would have rectified the holy sparks that had been scattered to the ends of the earth, and how would all of those spread and hidden among the *klipos* (literally, shells, meaning impure spiritual and material forces that surround and hide the holy sparks) been redeemed?

The answer he gives is, if Israel had never sinned, then their spiritual power would have been so great and mighty that they would work as a magnet to draw and attract all of the holy sparks from every end of the earth to their residence in the Holy Land. Then they would not have needed to wander to all of the far-off corners of the earth for that purpose. However, once they sinned, their holy powers were weakened, and they were not able to attract the holy sparks from afar. Thus, they needed to be exiled and wander from one place to another to lift up and repair these holy sparks. It is known in the name of the Holy Arizal that the purpose of the travels that the Israelites took to forty-two stations in the forty years in the desert wilderness was in order to separate the treasure from the refuse, and to soak up the holy sparks that were scattered among the *klipos*. According to this, we can understand that had the Israelites been worthy, they would have immediately entered the Holy Land and have been able to fix the holy sparks from there in their own place, since they would not have needed to be exiled to accomplish this. This is why it says "and God did not allow them to go by the path of the land of the Philistines" and to bring them right into the land immediately where they could have repaired the holy sparks from their own place, because "God said 'lest the people change their mind when they see war'." Through this change of mind against the Will of God, they will damage their holiness and again need to wander in order to rectify the holy sparks. Therefore "God caused them to go a round-about path into the desert" and through the forty-two stations of their wandering they rectified the holy sparks.

(Divrei Yoel)

"And (Pharaoh) said, 'what is this we have done? For we have sent Israel away from serving us!"

Rashi explains that Pharaoh was upset about the money the Egyptians had lent the Israelites. In order to understand this, we must first understand the statement of our Sages that was codified in the Shulchan Aruch (Code of Jewish Law), that it is forbidden to receive charity from heathens. This is learned from the Scripture "when its branches are dried out, it will be broken off" (Isaiah 27:11). Rashi explains that this means that when the merit the heathens have is finished, then their "moisture has been dried out". If we accept charity from them, this will give them new merit and energy.

Through this, we can understand Pharaoh's mistake, because even though God showed Pharaoh His amazing wonders through the plagues, to the point where Pharaoh was forced to send the Hebrews away, he thought that he was punished because of his lack of merit. But once the Egyptians had lent the Israelites gold and silver utensils, he thought that the Egyptians had gained new merits which would protect them from their punishment and their suffering. This is what Scripture tells us that "Pharaoh's heart was turned around... and he said 'what is this we have done? For we have sent Israel away from serving us!'", to which Rashi comments "because of the money Egypt lent them". This means that the reason that Pharaoh's heart had been turned around and he felt confident enough to pursue them was because he assumed that he could rely upon the spiritual power of this act of charity to be saved from punishment.
(Divrei Yoel)

Parshas Yisro

"And He said to Moses"

The Midrash tells us that God said to Moses "I am He who spoke and the world came to be. This man (Jethro) who comes to Me comes only to convert for the sake of Heaven. Thus, you should bring him close and not chase him away to be distant."

One could explain this according to the famous story brought in the Talmud about a gentile who came to Shammai to convert. Shammai chased him away, (because he asked to be taught the entire Torah while standing on one foot). He then came to Hillel, and was accepted to convert (as Hillel told him that the Torah tells us not to do to others what one dislikes himself, and that the rest is commentary). Tosafos asks, how could Hillel have accepted him? We are taught that we only accept converts if they are very persistent to convert. The answer is that Hillel knew (by Divine inspiration) that in the end they would be perfect converts, as happened in the end. Until here are the words of the Tosafos.

Jethro came from the nations of the world, and when he came to convert it would have been

proper according to the strict law to distance him first, as is the law of a heathen who wishes to convert. It is possible that Moses had a doubt whether to accept him, as it was possible that perhaps Jethro's intent was not for the sake of Heaven, and maybe he intended only so he could eat at the tables of kings (i.e. become wealthy). The doubt remained until God told him according to the laws of how to deal with people from the nations of the world who wish to convert, "therefore you should bring him close and not push him to be far away", similar to the story of Hillel. Immediately, "and Moses went out to greet his father-in-law."
(Divrei Yoel)

Parshas Mishpatim

"And these are the ordinances you shall set before them."

It seems fitting before I explain this verse, I should first bring my explanation for the scripture

"Happy is the man who God chastises, and from Your Torah he studies".

The Midrash tells us that when the Israelites heard the chapters of Scripture describing the laws of leprosy, they were afraid. God told them not to fear, for He said that these plagues "were for the heathen nations of the world, but I only wish to give to you to eat and to drink and to toil in the study of Torah." The Israelites feared that the plagues would actually come upon them physically, and God consoled them, giving them the advice that if they wish to be spared from these plagues they should study the Holy Torah. If the Israelites study the laws of leprosy, it is considered as if they suffered from it, thus they do not need to receive the plague physically. However, the heathens are not blessed by the power of the Torah, so they cannot be saved by study (without becoming Jewish).

This is the meaning of the verse "Happy is the man who God chastises", and then the scripture describes the suffering it is referring to, "and from Your Torah he studies." This means that the suffering does not come upon the person physically, God forbid, but rather that he fulfills his obligation of suffering through Torah study.

In this way, we can explain "and these are the ordinances" that this is hinting to the laws and their punishments, "that you should set before them", as if to say that you can fulfill the obligation to suffer according to the Torah's laws of punishment for sins through study and not in actual physical suffering. (Divrei Yoel)

Parshas Terumah

"And make for Me a Sanctuary and I will dwell within them"

It is well known that the Toldos Yaakov Yosef asked how this mitzvah can be fulfilled at all times. We can answer that it is possible to fulfill this mitzvah of building a tabernacle for God's presence to dwell at all times, because when one sets aside a place to study Torah, it is considered before God as if he built a portion of the Holy Temple. This is because, in the future, this place will be set in with the place of the Temple, thus it is considered as if one already built part of the

Temple. This is so, because God transcends time. Thus, past, present, and future are all one with God. It is only by our perception that there can be considered measures of time, placing the building of the Third Temple into the future, thus this portion will be brought to the Land of Israel in the future from our point of view. However, in God's eyes, there is no such thing as present or future, for all is before Him in one moment, as He transcends time. Thus, it is automatically and immediately considered as if it is already set there in Jerusalem.

(Divrei Yoel)

Parshas Tetzaveh

"And you shall command the Children of Israel, and you shall take for yourself pure olive oil, crushed to bring light, to bring up a constant lamp."

This can be explained according to what our Sages expounded in Toras Kohanim on the words "Before the Lord constantly" that "constantly" means even on the Sabbath. We already explained that God is hinting in His saying "and you shall command" that it means the future, for then Moses our teacher will return to be the leader of Israel, and he will command the Children of Israel to light the lamps in the Third Temple.

The Talmud teaches (Sanhedrin 97a) that in the future it will be a day that is totally Sabbath. Therefore, if it were not revealed to us in Scripture that the commandment to light the Menorah would override the Sabbath, we would find that the entire concept of kindling the Menorah would not apply in the future. Then we would have a difficulty, and we would ask how could the Scripture say "And you shall command the children of Israel", that Moses would command us to light the lamps in the future in the time of the Redemption. Therefore the Scripture writes immediately "to bring up a 'constant' lamp", to expound from those very words that this

applies even on the Sabbath (and even in the future time which will be only Sabbath).
(Divrei Yoel)

PARSHAS KI SISA

"And the Lord said to Moses, saying 'only you should keep My Sabbaths'..."

It is cited in the Mechilta that "and the Lord said to Moses saying" indicates that this statement did not come through and angel nor a messenger, but rather from God Himself. It would seem that we could explain this inasmuch as our Sages said that "there is no reward for a mitzvah in this world". The Commentators find this difficult, inasmuch as we know that God keeps the laws of the Torah, and the Torah itself says "you should give a worker's wages on the same day". Therefore, we find that when one sends a messenger to pay his workers, he is not violating the prohibition against paying them late.

It is known that 611 mitzvos were commanded to us by Moses, and only the first two commandments were heard directly by us from God's mouth. It is written in "Yismach Moshe" that when Moses would use the word "ko" (i.e. "thus says God"), he was speaking from his own voice and it was considered as being delivered by a messenger. However, when he said "*zeh*" (i.e. "this is the Word") that God was speaking through Moses's throat, thus we had the Word directly from God Himself.

Our Sages say that "anyone who enjoys his celebration of the Sabbath is given an inheritance without boundaries, and he is given all of the requests of his heart". Therefore, in the mitzvah of Shabbos, Moses used the term "*zeh hadavar*" ("this is the Word"), because it was God Himself who commanded us about the Sabbath, and not through a messenger. Thus, as we said above, we receive our reward for keeping the Sabbath in This World.

Through this, we can explain the words of the Mechilta, "and the Lord said to Moses, saying" means that it was not through an angel, and not through a messenger, because the word "saying" indicates that it was directly said to the Israelites, and not through the level of an angel as He did

with the other commandments. Rather, the mitzvah of Shabbos is different from the other mitzvos, as it was said in a level of "this is the Word", which leads to us receiving the reward for keeping Shabbos in This World.
(Divrei Yoel)

PARSHAS VAYAKHEL

"And Moses gathered"

It appears that we can explain this according to what the Turei Zahav writes on the statement of our Sages that concerning "one who observes the Sabbath according to its laws, even if he worshipped idols like the generation of Enosh, he is forgiven" that this is through teshuvah (repentance - i.e., the Sabbath observance is not sufficient to attain atonement without repentance). Thus, in order to attain full atonement for their sin (of making the golden calf), the Israelites needed to repent out of love for God, in order to transform their intentional sins into merits. Therefore, the Yismach Moshe writes, that public repentance by the masses is considered to be repentance out of love.

According to this, we can explain the above Scripture, because the word "these" hints to the sin of the golden calf, when it was said "these are your gods, o Israel". Therefore, Scripture lets us know here "and Moses gathered the entire congregation of the Children of Israel", and by the power of his holy words he woke them up to repent for the act of making the golden calf. "And he said to them, 'these' are the words", meaning the words that were said to the golden calf "these are your gods, o Israel". "That the Lord commanded to 'do them'," meaning that in the power of repentance, they will make this sin into mitzvos "that the Lord commanded", because they turned around for them from intentional sins into merits.

And do not wonder how all of Israel reached the level of "repentance out of love" until their sins were turned into merits. That is why the Scripture said "and Moses gathered all of the congregation of the Children of Israel", and when they are all assembled together it helps that the merit of public repentance by the masses can turn their sins around into merits, even if they only repent out of fear.

(Divrei Yoel)

"And Moses gathered"

In the beginning of this Parshah, the Holy Zohar cites that "God said, 'from now on, the construction of the Tabernacle will only be conducted by the Israelites alone,' immediately we see 'and Moses gathered'. This is because there was the mixed multitude among them, (who had worshipped the golden calf), so Moses needed to gather them and to separate them from among them". Until here are the words of the Holy Zohar.

It seems from the words of the Holy Zohar that inasmuch as they were forbidden to take money to build the Tabernacle from the Mixed Multitude, we can say something novel: Just as Moses commanded them not to take a donation from the Mixed Multitude toward the building of the Tabernacle because they worshipped idolatry when they made the golden calf, so too he commanded them not to take money for the needs of the Tabernacle from Sabbath desecrators. The reason for this is explained in the holy Hasidic literature. This concept is particularly expanded upon in the holy book "Agra D'Kallah" in Parshas Shoftim, "that we are not to derive benefit from money that has its source from people who are not fit, inasmuch as the power of one who provides energy to another is found in the one affected by this action. Thus, money taken from a bad source will make a bad impact on the one who receives it". Until here are the words of the Agra D'Kallah.

If this is so, then all the more so and all the more so then we cannot build the Tabernacle, which is the place where the Divine Presence of God dwells, from money that comes from a source that is not pure. This is because the Tabernacle is the place from which in its path all of the good influence comes to Israel, and money that is not kosher can damage the conduits of this outpouring of blessing.

According to this, we can possibly explain the words of Rashi, z"l, that the "warning to observe the Sabbath precede the building of the Tabernacle, to teach that the building of the

Tabernacle does not over ride the Sabbath". This means that we should not think to take money from Sabbath desecrators to build the Tabernacle. Thus the warning to observe the Sabbath precedes the building of the Tabernacle, in order to ward them how serious the Sabbath is, and that we may not take money from Sabbath desecrators for the needs of the Tabernacle.

(Divrei Yoel)

"And Moses gathered"

To return to our subject, to explain the words of the Holy Zohar, that we know that the Mixed Multitude caused the Israelites to stumble in the matter of the golden calf, as it is cited in the Holy Zohar that they made the calf and tempted the Israelites to worship it. The entire time that they were found among the children of Israel, and they had a connection with them, it was not possible to make unity among the upright members of Israel, which is why "Moses gathered the entire congregation of the Children of Israel," etc. The Zohar explains that Moses chose them out and separated them from the Mixed Multitude, in order that they should be able to guard their own identity and unity among themselves. Thus, it was necessary to separate them from the Mixed Multitude, who were like a painful thorn that brought about strife among Israel. Only by separating from the Mixed Multitude was it possible to make a proper gathering which made true friendship and fellowship possible among the pious Israelites.

(Divrei Yoel)

"These are the things that the LORD commanded to do them. Six days work will be done, and on the seventh day it will be holy to you."

The Kli Yakar asks why does it say "work will be done"? It should have said "you shall do work". The words "work will be done" seem to indicate that the work will be done on its own. We can explain this based on what is stated in the Holy Zohar (Parshas Yisro), "all blessings above and below are dependent upon the Seventh Day." One should study that portion, because it explains that through the observance of the Sabbath according to its laws, the other six days of the week are blessed Above. It is from that blessing that all six days of the work week are blessed. Thus, we see that our success during the six working days is dependent upon proper Sabbath observance according to all of its laws.

Through this, we can explain our subject matter, inasmuch as it is written "these are the things that the Lord commanded to do them", which refers to the observance of the Sabbath that follows this portion. This is seen in the teachings of our Sages (see Talmud Shabbos 97b). In any event, we see that God wanted us to know by His words "to do them" that despite the fact that Sabbath observance is basically the command not to do work, but because we are commanded here right away to make the Tabernacle, the work that we do during the six days of the work week are only possible to be completed above through Sabbath observance, as we said above. Thus, Scripture states "to do them", which also indicates the building of the Tabernacle as well. Through this, we fulfill "these are the things that the Lord commanded" by Sabbath observance, which is to do them, and thus bless the work of building the Tabernacle. Scripture explains that "six days work will be done, and on the seventh day will be a restful Sabbath" which means that through

Sabbath observance, the work will be done on its own in the six days above. All that a person needs to do during the six days of the work week is to fulfill them in actuality, by which the work is finished by the potential energy generated by the observance of the previous Sabbath, for through it are the six days blessed Above, and they pour down influence of blessing and success in what a person does during the six work days below. (Divrei Yoel)

PARSHAS PEKUDEI

"These are the accounts of the Tabernacle, the Tabernacle of Testimony."

Rashi explains why the word "Tabernacle" appears twice. He said it hints to the Temple that was temporary, inasmuch as it was destroyed twice due to the sins of Israel. The commentators ask how is this connected to the accounts of the donations given to the Tabernacle (which applies only to the Wilderness Tabernacle), rather than when God commanded the building of the

Tabernacle (which really is connected to the future Temple as well)?

It appears that we can answer this according to that which is cited in the Holy Zohar, which God commanded to take donations for the Tabernacle only from the righteous servants of the Lord, who serve God with all of their heart and all of their soul. However, since they did not want to embarrass the others, they accepted silver donations from all of Israel. A miracle occurred that there was enough to build the Tabernacle from the portion of the righteous people, because God sent them a blessing. The portion of the other donors was left over, and they were saddened and depressed over that, because they saw that God did not want their donations. In order to relieve their worries, God commanded that the Temple should be built from the left-over money (as is cited in the Yalkut).

God said to Moses that they should make a Tabernacle for the words from the leftovers, and the commentators write that the intent was to build a study hall to learn Torah, as a house of Torah study is also called a small Temple.

It is taught in the Talmud (Megillah 29a) that the synagogues and study halls outside of the Diaspora are destined in the future to be set in the Land of Israel. This is how the Maharsh"a explains the verse in Psalms "the built Jerusalem is like a city that is connected together". We know that in the future the Temple will be as big as all of Jerusalem. He says that the reason is because the future built-up Jerusalem will have the Temple being connected of the places of the Synagogues that were in this world. (Until here are the words of the Maharsh"a).

It is clear that today's synagogues will be set into the place of the Temple in the future. If this is the case, then this is how the donors will be comforted, because even if their donations will not be used to build the Tabernacle, in any event it will be destined that the study halls that they built will be set into the place of the Holy Temple.

Through this, we can understand why this hint is found here. It is because through the fact that God gave an accounting of the donations of the Tabernacle, it was revealed to Israel that there was money leftover from the donations. Thus, they were saddened, and they needed to be comforted by building halls of Torah study with their donations. And those study halls are destined to be set into the place of the Holy Temple in the future. Thus, they also have a portion in God's Tabernacle. Thus, they needed to know that two Temples were destined to be destroyed, and that the Third Holy Temple will stand forever, and will be built with their synagogues and study halls. Thus, they were worthy to have a connection to the Holy Temple, which would be connected to their study halls and synagogues that were built by their donations.

(Divrei Yoel)

"These are the accounts of the Tabernacle that were accounted for by the mouth of Moses through the hand of Ithamar"

It seems that we can explain this based on what the Ohr HaChayim HaKadosh wrote in Parshas Vayakhel on the Scripture "and the work was enough... and too much". It seems to be difficult for us to understand, for this seems to indicate two opposites. If it was "enough", it was not "too much"; and if it was "too much", that is not called "enough". It is possible that Scripture is informing us here of the love that God has in His Eyes for the Children of Israel, inasmuch as the Israelites brought more than the necessary amount to build the Tabernacle. Thus, God was concerned for the respect due to each person who worked hard to bring everything needed for the House of the Lord in the building of the Tabernacle. This is the meaning of the Scripture "and the work that they brought was enough", that nothing was lacking and also nothing was left over. Even though the truth was that there was too much, but a miracle occurred that nothing was left over. However, through this we can understand that it would simply not be possible to give a proper accounting of the donations, because everything that was brought was miraculously incorporated into the Tabernacle, more than was necessary to be used to build the Tabernacle according to the calculations. However, it was only Ithamar with his Divine inspiration who was able to understand this calculation as well. This is the meaning of "that was accounted by the mouth of Moses", because he had called other accountants to calculate this, but he did not call simple people, because they would not be able to understand this calculation on their own. This was only able to be calculated by Ithamar, who was able to understand this calculation through his Divine inspiration.

(Divrei Yoel)

LEVITICUS/VAYIKRA

PARSHAS VAYIKRA

"And He called to Moses, and the LORD said to him" (Leviticus 1:1)

It seems that we can explain this according to the statement of our Sages, of blessed memory, "The LORD, the LORD" means "I am He before someone commits a sin, and I am He after the person has sinned and then repented." The Rosh asks why does someone need God's Mercy (indicated by the Name "Hashem" or "the LORD) before one commits a sin? It seems that we can explain this according to the statement of the Sages that "A person's desires would overcome him all day, except if God did not help him, he would not be able to resist."

This means that, without God's Help, it is impossible for a person to stand up against the desire to do evil, because the desire is stronger than the person. It is only from the Kindness of the Creator, Who is holding a person's hand to stand up strong in the war against the Yetzer Hara (desire to do evil). This is how we can answer the question of the Rosh as to what Divine Mercy a person needs before a sin, that we need God's Mercy to stand up against the against our wicked enemy, the Yetzer Hara, who is constantly wickedly pursuing us to try to cause us to stumble in sin. This is why the beginning of the passage explaining the Sacrifices begins with "And the Lord spoke to him", because Scripture intends to teach us that there is a path before a man to conquer his desires and to be saved from sin. A person should not say that this is not within the realm of possibility, inasmuch as it is not possible for a person to be victorious over the desire to do evil that burns within him like a fire. This is why God's special Name is mentioned in the beginning of the passage, to teach us that the Lord in His Mercy will help a person to battle against his desires, and God will not abandon him into the hand of sin.

(Divrei Yoel)

"And He called unto Moses"

Rashi says "go and say to them words of rebuke and comfort, for your sakes, He speaks with me".

We can explain this according to what the Kedushas Levi wrote to explain the words of the Hagadah, "and if He had brought us before Mount Sinai, and did not give us the Torah, it would have been enough" that when the Children of Israel came to Mount Sinai, their impurity of the original sin left them and their limbs were purified until they understood all of the Torah on their own. Therefore, according to what they saw from His Wisdom, because they would not always stand on that high level, therefore God commanded them immediately the mitzvos of the Torah. Now we can understand the meaning of what Rashi says "go and say to them words of rebuke and comfort for your sakes God speaks with me" because all of the commandments were only for your sakes because you sinned with the golden calf, and through this the Yetzer Hara returned to rule over them. But Moses did not require commandments because he always remained on this holy level and he understood all of the words of this Torah on his own.

(Divrei Yoel)

"When a man takes from you"

We could also say the following to explain the intentions of Rashi, z"l, "go and tell them words of rebuke, 'it is for your sakes He speaks with me'." Also, we can explain this that is cited in the Yalkut "it is possible that He was speaking to him for his own sake, thus Scripture tells us that He was speaking to him for the sake of Israel and not for his own sake". This is very surprising. It is known that the commandments of the Sacrifices were not said for Moses' sake, but rather for the needs of Israel.

In Midrash Rabbah (Leviticus Rabbah 1:2), it is cited that "Rabbi Abahu opened his discourse saying that 'Return ye who sit in His Shadow' (Hosea 14), refers to the converts, who come to shelter themselves in the Shadow of God." This needs to be explained, why does this discourse come to praise converts? What does this have to do with the passages explaining Sacrifices? It would seem that these two things have nothing to do with each other at all.

In Midrash Rabbah, Parshas Tzav (Leviticus Rabbah 9:8), it is cited that "Rabbi Acha said a parable concerning a king... of which we can learn that once Israel heard the passages of the Sacrifices, they were frightened. Moses told them, do not be afraid. Busy yourselves with Torah study, and you do not have to be afraid of all of these things. This is why it is written 'this is the Torah of the burnt offering, this is the Torah of the meal offering'." This is also a wonder, why would the Israelites be frightened when they hear the passages of the Sacrifices?

It seems that we can explain the concept inasmuch as the Midrash Toras Kohanim explains the verse "when a man offers" (Leviticus 1:2) that the word "man" comes to include the converts. The Sefer Korban Aharon asks, why does Scripture need to tell us that Converts can bring Sacrifices just the same as natural born Israelites? We known that the Talmud teaches (Chullin 13b) that we except Sacrifices even from gentiles. He answers that we might think that converts are excluded, because now they are part of Israel, and we see that Scripture seems to exclude some Israelites, as it says "when a man offers from you", that "from you" indicates that not all of you are included, thus Scripture needed to specifically include converts so we should know that they can also bring sacrifices. Until here are the words of the Korban Aharon. The Or HaChayim HaKadosh pushes away the answer of the Korban Aharon, see there.

It seems to me that Scripture needed to specifically include Converts because the Talmud says (Chullin 5a) that by the Scripture stating "from you" and not "all of you", it comes to exclude an apostate Jew, (as we do not accept a voluntary donation of a sacrifice from an apostate Jew). Then it says "I have made a distinction from you but not from the gentile nations". (To which Rashi explains that this Scripture only excludes Israelites and not Gentiles, because Gentiles can also bring voluntary sacrifices like Israelites, as it is written "a man, a man from the house of Israel, who offers" [Leviticus 23], which we learn that the extra word "a man" comes to include the Gentiles, who can make pledges and offer voluntary sacrifices just as Israelites may. However, Scripture does not exclude any gentiles, because it does not say "from the men when he offers a sacrifices", which would indicate that some gentiles are excluded, [but the verse simply states "a man", indicating "any man"]. Thus, we see from this that the exclusivity only applies to Israelites, inasmuch as among Israel, only the kosher Israelites may bring, but not apostates. However, all Gentiles, no matter what their religion is, may pledge a sacrifice to the Temple and we accept it from them.) We find from the Talmud that we can accept sacrifices from most Jewish sinners, to help them to repent from their sins, but not from an apostate Jew who defiles wine libations and publicly desecrates the Sabbaths. Until here are the words of the Talmud.

It is clarified from this that Scripture only makes a distinction between the kosher people and the apostates among the Israelites as to who may offer a sacrifice, however among the gentiles we accept sacrifices even from their apostates. According to this, we can understand clearly why Scripture needed to state "a man" to include converts, because a convert is no longer a gentile at all in any manner, and is judged as an Israelite, even in this matter. This means that we do not accept sacrifices from apostate Jews who had converted to Judaism. Thus, the question of the Korban Aharon is not a question at all, as he asks if we know that we accept sacrifices even from gentiles, so it should be all the more so from converts, so why does Scripture need to tell us this that they can also offer sacrifices? But rather, they are judged the same as Israelites even in this matter, that we do not accept sacrifices from apostates who violate the Sabbath publicly and defile wine libations.

However, this is the very concept, that the Torah is always stricter with Israelites than with gentiles, as we need to know why we do not accept from the Jewish apostates. It seems that there are two reasons for this thing. One is according to what the Ohr HaChaim HaKadosh wrote in the beginning of Parshas Chukas as to the reason why the Sages say (Talmud Yevamos 61a) that Jewish corpses impart impurity but gentile corpses do not. He said that we can compare this to two containers, one filled with honey and the other filled with garbage. When you put them both outside, the flies and bugs mostly gather to the honey, while the garbage pail only attracts a few flies. So too, when a Jew's soul leaves his body when he dies, the body is emptied that was filled with the sweetest holiness, thus the *klipos* (impure forces) gather to it without measure, because they desire to attach themselves to holiness. Until here are the words of the Ohr HaChaim HaKadosh. See there as he elaborates his pleasant words.

Through this we can find a good reason why the Torah was stricter with a Jewish heretic than with a gentile heretic. Because the Jew separated himself from the Torah, thus the powers of impurity immensely grab on to him to cause him to sin. That is why his sacrifice is not pleasing to God. This is not the case with a gentile idolater or heretic, because the klipos do not attach themselves to him so much.

There is another great reason for this, as we know that Maimonides, z"l, writes that it is easier to learn from the wicked deeds of an evil Jew than from the wicked deeds of an evil gentile, because Jews generally do not feel a natural connection to gentiles. Despite this, we see that the Sages enacted many fences and decreed many forms of separation in order that we should not learn from heathens (Talmud Bava Metzia 71a). In any event, this is why we are more lenient with a gentile heretic than with a Jewish apostate, as we accept sacrifices from all gentiles, because we are not worried that we might learn from their ways as we are worried about learning from an apostate Jew.

We can derive from this that the Scriptural passages teaching about the Sacrifices pierce our emotions and enter down to the deepest chambers of our hearts, because from them we can hear how far these things reach, and how great is the power of impurity attached to wicked Jews. We also see how far we are obligated to separate ourselves from them, that we should not come to learn from their ways, even to the point where the Torah forbids accepting sacrifices from them because of this worry. Through this we can explain how the Israelites were afraid when they heard the chapters of the Sacrifices, because they saw how Scripture differentiates between a Jewish heretic and a gentile heretic, as our Sages taught that the verse "when a person among you offers a sacrifice", that I make a distinction "among you" and not among the heathens. They were informed about how the powers of impurity strongly desire to attach themselves to Israel, and thus their hearts trembled when they realized how far a person could fall, if he corrupts his deeds. Since they were not on the level of the perfectly righteous, they were gripped with trembling fear, for perhaps their sins would cause them to fall into oblivion through the forces of impurity. Thus, Moses answered them that "if you busy yourselves with the study Torah, you do not need to fear from any of this", because the Torah protects us and rescues us from the devil and his forces that they cannot conquer us.

And according to what we explained that Scripture comes to exclude accepting Sacrifices from apostate Jews, lest we learn from their ways, we can come to elucidate the teachings of the Midrash Toras Kohanim (as we mentioned in the first question) that God spoke to Moses for the sake of Israel and not for his own sake, because the entire prohibition against accepting sacrifices from apostate Jews was only for the benefit of the Jewish people, that they should not come to learn from the ways of the heretics. However, since Moses was on such a high level, he did not need to have such a decree, because we were not worried that Moses might have learned from their ways, because he was a fundamentally and totally righteous person, (as in "the righteous person is the foundation of the world"), and all of the winds of the world would not budge him from his place. This is what the Toras Kohanim means that God was speaking to Moses for the needs of Israel and not for his own needs, because on his high level Moses did not need the prohibition against accepting offerings and donations from Jewish heretics. This thing was only forbidden because of the Israelites, that they should not come to learn from the ways of the heretics.

And this also explains Rashi's intent in what it says "go and say words of rebuke, for your sakes He speaks with me", that this warning not to accept sacrifices from Jewish apostates was only "for your sakes", because your imperfections make you vulnerable to learning from their ways. These words of rebuke conquer a person's heart to repent, when they see how their sins have caused them to fall from a high level.

And from this explains the Midrash Rabbah (quoted in the second question), that this teaching stated that "return ye who sit in His Shadow" refers to converts. This scriptural passage proves again how Converts are judged as being totally

Jewish in all ways, even in the stringency that the Torah applies to Israelites and not to Gentiles that we do not accept sacrifices from Jewish apostates, that it includes both born Jews and converts. Therefore, this Midrash expounds upon the praise of converts. This is because this gives us the teaching that a convert is totally Jewish in all ways, thus if a converted Jew becomes an apostate, we have to worry that other Jews would learn from their ways, because the forces of impurity attach to them more than they do to a gentile heretic, because a convert has become sanctified with the holiness of Israel.
(Divrei Yoel - Parshas Vayikra p. 60-62)

PARSHAS TZAV

"And the Lord spoke to Moses saying, 'command Aaron and his sons, saying to them this is the Law of the Burnt Offering'"

It seems that since the word "saying" is used twice, one would seem to be extra. It seems that we know that we learn from the words "this is the Law of the Burnt Offering" that anyone who studies that laws of the Burnt Offering it is considered as if he had offered a Burnt Offering. One might think that only by studying the laws of the Burnt Offering in depth and understanding all of its laws that the study would be considered in place of an actual offering. One would assume this because the Sages use the term "anyone who toils in the study of the laws of the burnt offering", that this indicates that one needs to engage in difficult study to understand and derive the laws. But what is one to do if his mind is not tuned for this, and he does not have the energy to study the laws to find their intricacies? This is certainly the case in the later generations up to today, as our Sages already taught "in the past, when money was available more easily, men desired to hear laws of Mishnah and Halachah. However, today, as the financial situation is more difficult, people only want to hear words of blessing and Agadah." If this is the case, then who would study the laws of the burnt offering? And if they merely learn and read the words without understanding them, then it would seem that this learning would not be considered like a sacrifice. This is why the Scripture says the word "saying" an extra time, to teach that we are obligated to study the passages of the Sacrifices even by mere recitation, without deep understanding of the laws. Even if one does not understand the laws deeply, the recitation is considered in place of a Sacrifice.

(Divrei Yoel)

"And this is the Torah of the Burnt Offering"

The Midrash says "Rabbi Yosi ben Kisma's students asked him, 'when will the Messiah son of David come?', he answered 'this is the Torah of the burnt offering'." We can explain this by first mentioning what the Noam Elimelech wrote on the verse "and from then I came to speak in Your Name", that since we are in this bitter Exile, where our sufferings cause Him pain, as the Shechinah (Divine Presence of God) is Exiled with us, we should only worry about the Exile of the Shechinah and not think about our suffering at all, but only the suffering and Exile of the Shechinah. If this was our entire focus, which all of our pain was only because of the pain of the Shechinah and not our own suffering, then we would have certainly been redeemed immediately. However, we are mere flesh, and we are not able to withstand our pain and suffering in our persecutions, thus our Exile is prolonged... If there were one righteous person like this, who ignored his own pain and only focused on the pain of the Shechinah, then he could save the entire world from Exile. Until here are the words of the Noam Elimelech.

With this, we can explain why when Rabbi Yosi ben Kisma's disciples asked when the Messiah son of David would come; he answered "This is the Torah of the Burnt Offering". Because just as the Burnt Offering is entire consumed by the fire, totally going up to God without any portion remaining for people to consume, so too it would be if there were one righteous person who only felt pain from the Exile of the Shechinah, and not think at all about human suffering on the human level, then the Redemption would come immediately.

(Divrei Yoel)

"This is the Torah of the Burnt Offering"

In Midrash Pliah, Rabbi Yosi ben Kisma's students asked him "when will the Messiah son of

David come" to which he answered them "this is the Torah of the Burnt Offering".

It is known that there is a tradition from my great-grandfather the Yismach Moshe, zt"l, who received a direct tradition from one person to the next all the way back to Elijah the Prophet, that the meaning of the Talmudic passage (Sanhedrin 97a) "The Messiah son of David will not come until the prutah (a small coin, like a penny) leaves the pocket" is that selfishness (the word "prutah" is related to the word "prat" or "individual") should leave the pocket of the heart, that we should not focus on individual selfish concerns but rather focus on the collective needs of the Jewish people. For this one needs a true and trustworthy heart, so one would not be concerned for anything selfish but rather the collective needs of others.

In any event, in order to be worthy to this, one needs a perfectly pure heart, so one does not focus on selfishness but rather altruism. This is very difficult, but when one is worthy to this, he is worthy to the Redemption. This is what Rabbi Yosi ben Kisma answered his disciples' question of "when will the Messiah son of David come?" to

which he answered "this is the Torah of the Burnt Offering". This is where the rectification of the heart lies, for the burnt offering atones for the thoughts of the heart. If you look into this mitzvah, you will see how the Redemption can come.
(Divrei Yoel)

PARSHAS SHMINI

"And Moses said to Aaron, draw near to the altar and make your sin offering and your burnt offering, and atone for you and for the people, and make the sacrifice of the people and atone for them."

One may ask, why did Aaron need to atone for the people? The people brought their own sacrifice to atone for themselves, as it is written "and make the sacrifice if the people and atone for them". One might say that Aaron the Priest did not need atonement for himself, because his intentions during the incident of the Golden Calf were for the Sake of Heaven, as the Midrash teaches that he said "it is better that the blame should rest upon mean and not upon all Israel". However, he did need atonement inasmuch as the Israelites stumbled through their associations with the members of the Mixed Multitude who made the Calf. This association was caused by virtue of the fact that they learned the ways of Peace from Aaron, thus this damage came to them and they needed atonement. This is the meaning of the Scripture "And atone for you and for the people", as if to say that the reason you need atonement is for yourself, is because the sin of the nation touched you as well, because they stumbled by associating themselves with wicked people. However, Aaron, in and of himself, was perfect and clean of any sin or iniquity, because he himself only used the ways of Peace to associate himself with pious, God-fearing people.

(Divrei Yoel)

"And Moses said to Aaron, draw near to the Altar"

Rashi explains that Aaron was ashamed and afraid to come close, thus Moses said to him "why are you ashamed? This is what you were chosen for." It seems that we can explain this through the known teaching of the Arizal, that the Levites of today will be the Priests in the future. This was the mistake of Korah, who thought that the world had already been perfected and the Messianic era had arrived, thus he had become a Kohen (priest). Through this we can understand what our Sages said that Moses was pained when God told him "and you should bring your brother Aaron close to you", that he was pained as he realized that Israel had not yet been worthy to the full Rectification, and that they were destined to go from one exile to the next, and suffer tremendous and horrible persecutions, thus was his heart downtrodden. When he saw the low level that Israel would reach in the End of Days, Moses was worried for them, for how could they be redeemed from such a terribly low level? Thus, God answered him that the power of the Holy Torah that the Israelites had accepted would stand for them to shield and protect them at every time and era, and in the merit of the Torah would Israel leave the Exile, even in the lowest level that they are given into.

In this way, we can explain why Aaron was ashamed to draw near to the altar, because Aaron knew that when the world would be fixed, the Levites would become the Priests. This is why he was ashamed, because he was only going to be a Priest in this world, but in the future, he would be pushed out of his priesthood. If so, then it shows that he is not properly whole in his service to God, if so, why should be considered to stand and minister at God's altar? Thus, Moses answered him that it is indeed true that in the future, the Levites would become Priests, but in any event, the Priests would also remain Priests. Thus, Aaron would remain in his station and minister as the High Priest in the future, just as he served in the Tabernacle. This is because we have a general rule that we go up in holiness and do not go down. This is why Moses told Aaron "this is why you were chosen", meaning that he would serve as High Priest in the future. Thus, he would have no reason to be ashamed, as the priesthood would not cease from him in the future.

(Divrei Yoel)

PARSHAS SAZRIA

"When a woman gives birth"

The Midrash Rabbah teaches that this is what is written "I formed you first and last", meaning that if a person is worthy, he is told that he was the most important creation, but if not he is told that a mosquito came before him. It is difficult to understand how the situation can change if a man is worthy or not? It seems that we can explain this based on what the Ohr HaChaim HaKadosh wrote, that when the world was created, God only created enough power in the world to exist for six days, for a reason known to Him. Then, God, in His Wisdom, created the Sabbath. For it was on that day that the soul returned to the world and imbued enough energy to exist for another six days, and so it repeats every week. This is the reason that the Torah says "and on the eighth day ye shall circumcise the flesh of his foreskin", that the circumcision should be postponed until the eighth day, as our Sages teach that this is in order that the child should have strength. This is also the same thing, in the way we explained, that a Sabbath should pass in his lifetime, thus giving him the live-giving soul power that is poured into the world on the Sabbath day, as is known. Then the child would be sustained in life. Until here are his words.

According to this, we can understand the connection that this Midrash is making here. For the Torah says "and on the eighth day, the flesh of his foreskin shall be circumcised", in order that a Sabbath should pass by upon his lifetime and he would receive the life-giving soul power through the Sabbath. Thus, if a person is worthy to fulfill the commandments of God, and observe the Sabbath according to its laws, thus he is worthy to be told that he is the most important Creation of God. This is because without human beings keeping the Sabbath, the world would not have continued to exist. Thus, we see that the rest of Creation is subordinate to the human being who observes the Sabbath and they are all secondary to him, for their entire existence depends on his deeds. If one is not worthy, meaning he does not observe the Sabbath according to its laws, then he is told that a mosquito preceded him, because that is the fact that the human being was the last creation made chronologically.

(Divrei Yoel)

PARSHAS METZORAH

"This shall be the Torah of the leper on the day of his purification"

It is possible that we can explain this by first explaining the Scripture "Happy is the man who God punishes, and from Your Torah does he learn". Our Sages teach that anyone who studies the laws of the burnt offering is considered as if he brought a burnt offering. Thus, as it is possible to fulfill the obligation to bring a sacrifice through studying the Bible passage about it, as it is written "and the offering of our lips shall pay instead of bulls" (Hosea), so too if a person is worthy then if he is decreed to suffer he could fulfill that decree through Torah study, through studying the passages of the plagues of leprosy and other forms of suffering, and then it is considered as if he had actually suffered those pains physically. This is what is written "happy is the man who God punishes", when is it a praise to a person if God punishes him? In the manner of "and from Your Torah he learns", as if to say that he fulfills his obligatory suffering through Torah study and not through actual physical suffering. This is the meaning of "This shall be the 'Torah' of the

Leper", meaning that he will continue to exist through the "Torah" of the Leper, without actually suffering from physical leprosy, but rather only through studying the Torah of the Leper. And this is the meaning of "on the day of his purification", that if he purifies himself and accepts upon himself the yoke of the kingdom of heaven perfectly, then it is enough for him to study the Bible passage, and it is considered as if these plagues physically came upon him (thus cleansing him spiritually).
(Divrei Yoel)

PARSHAS ACHAREI

"And you shall not do like the deeds of the land of Canaan where I am bringing you"

It seems that we can say that we can explain this according to the words of our Sages that "the nations of the world have a special love for our Holy Land", and in ancient times all of the inhabitants of the world from one end to of the earth to the other had tremendous respect for the Land of Israel. All of the leaders and rulers of the

world desired to make their dwelling place within the Land, and to build beautiful towers and memorials to their own names for the sake of their own desires. Thus, the tremendous love that the nations of the world had for the Land of Israel was despised by God, because these heathens who dwelled in the Land committed all kinds of abominations, and defiled the Land with their evil deeds. Thus, God commanded to destroy, kill, and annihilate the seven Canaanite nations that inhabited the Land. It is possible that this is what the Scripture intends, that we should not do like the deeds of these wicked nations, to be lovers of the Land like them (for selfish and sinful reasons), for that is not what is to be done. Because loving the Land without Torah and Mitzvos is an abomination to us. The first and most important thing for the Israelite nation to do is to desire and yearn with all of their hearts to fulfill the mitzvos, and this is the only way for the love of the Land to enter their hearts, and in no other way.
(Divrei Yoel)

PARSHAS KEDOSHIM

"You shall be holy, for I am Holy"

In Midrash Toras Kohanim, it is cited that "if you make yourselves holy, I consider it as if you had sanctified Me". We can understand this based on the teaching of our Sages that "the Wicked Nebuchadnezzar went to conquer the entire world. God said, 'What caused this that I should help the cause of idolatry? The sins of Israel!" The explanation of this can be made according to the words of Rashi on the verse "and you shall serve other gods, wood and stone..." that is means that we will serve those who serve these idols, thus it is considered by Scripture as if we had served the idols. This is the same idea in how God gave power to the Wicked Nebuchadnezzar that, so to speak if it were possible to say, it could be considered that God Himself was serving these idols, because when one serves a person who worships idols it is as if one serves the idols. This is the meaning of "if you make yourselves holy" from sin, making you holy to the Lord your God, "I consider it as if you sanctified Me". This is because through the holiness of the Children of Israel keeping pure from sin, God Himself

becomes distanced from idolatry, because if we are not sinning, then He does not need to give kingship and power to idolaters.
(Divrei Yoel)

PARSHAS EMOR

"Say unto the Priests"

The Holy Zohar mentions "Rabbi Yosi said 'say unto the Priests' in a whisper". It would seem that we would ask, are the mitzvos a secret? Quite the opposite, the entire Torah is available to anyone like a desert is available to anyone, and anyone who wishes to learn Torah can come and learn. Thus, we need to ask, why was this mitzvah said in a whisper? It seems that we can first mention the words from my illustrious and holy ancestor, zt"l, in his book Yismach Moshe, where he points out that it is written "and he shall not become defiled from a soul among his people", with a letter "yud" at the beginning of the word "yitma" ("become defiled"), which indicates speaking to someone hidden (i.e. general speaking - i.e. we see it says "he" shall not become defiled). It would have seemed to be more fitting to say "you shall not become defiled", with a "tav" at the beginning of the word "titma", as when one speaks to someone (by saying "you" shall not). This is because all of the time in Scripture, God tells Moses the exact words meant to be said to Israel. Thus, since God commanded him "say unto the Priests", we would assume that God would want Moses to use this exact verbatim language to speak to the Priests. We can explain why God commanded Moses to warn the Priests with a "yud" (i.e. "he" instead of "you"), because in addition to the warning we also have here a blessing and a decree. The blessing and decree of a righteous person helps for good, as it says "and he will decree and say, and you will support it, and understand that this is true" (Job 22). This is a wonderful explanation, with God's help. Until here are his holy words.

It would seem that it is not clear to us what is the blessing hidden in this commandment? We might say that the intent is upon the future. This is what is cited in the Midrash Tanchuma (3) that because in this world a priest may be defiled for a dead person without anyone to take care of him (meis mitzvah). However, in the future they will never be defiled at all, because there will be no death in the future. Through this we can understand the meaning of the words of the Yismach Moshe, zt"l, because the Scripture is hinting to us in saying that "he will not be defiled for a soul" with a "yud" at the beginning of the word (saying "he" rather than "you"), because in the future we will no longer be defiled for the dead, because "death will be swallowed up forever". Because of this, this Scripture also hints to us the concept of the Resurrection of the Dead, which will be in the time of the future Redemption. This is the explanation of the words of the Holy Zohar "say unto the priests" in a whisper, because here we are hinting to things that will be at the End Times, which are words meant to be said in a whisper, as they are not meant to be revealed publicly.

(Divrei Yoel)

"And you shall count for yourselves from the morrow of the day of rest"

It is possible to explain this according to how the Yismach Moshe explained the Midrash that "Aaron's sacrifice was beloved by God like the sacrifice of the princes". This is because there is no Jew who does not have some time when he desires to do the will of his Maker and he sets it upon his heart to return to God. However, no piety is as strong as it is when it is first starting. After some time, one becomes cold-hearted and returns to how it was before. However, the people who are always growing (Bnei Aliyah) always feel that every moment is like the first moment, for at every moment it seems as if they are just starting to serve God. Thus, by such a person, there is no middle or end, only a constant beginning. Now, the sacrifices of the Princes that were at the dedication of the Sanctuary were certainly with tremendous enthusiasm, as they saw the Glory of God fill the Tabernacle. That was the first dedication. For sure this was very beloved before God. This is what the Midrash said about Aaron's sacrifice, which was twice every day, that it was beloved before God like the sacrifice of the Princes. This is the way of the Bnei Aliyah, by whom every moment is like the first time. Until here are the words of the Yismach Moshe.

Rabbi Aaron HaLevi wrote in Sefer HaChinuch that the reason for the commandment of counting the Omer was to show the tremendous love and desire that the Israelites have for the holy festival which is the season of the giving of our Torah. It goes so far that out of our tremendous love and desire for this holiday, we are counting the days and weeks, like a person who is waiting for an important thing, and our spirit becomes tired from waiting until we are worthy to have this important thing, thus we count the days that have already passed. According to this we can explain the Scripture "and you shall count fifty days", as Rabbi Aaron HaLevi writes that each day of counting the Omer should be focused on the main point of the fiftieth day. We might be worried, however, that if we always focus on that fiftieth day all throughout the entire time of counting the Omer, we might get cooled off from our enthusiasm, and once that fiftieth day finally comes we might not have that same enthusiasm burning in our hearts like a fire as we had at first. This is why Scripture warns "and you shall bring a new offering to the Lord", that this mitzvah should be like it is a brand new one in your eyes every day, then you will have enthusiasm and desire for the commandment as at the beginning.

(Divrei Yoel)

PARSHAS BEHAR

"When you come into the Land that I give to you, and the Land shall rest a Sabbath unto the Lord"

Some would say that it is know that our Sages said that Israel is exiled from their Land for the sin of violating the Sabbatical year. Then they abandon the Land and the Sabbaticals are fulfilled, as the Land is given her rest. It is also cited in the Midrash Tanchuma that God said to Moses "if you do not want Israel to be exiled, warn them to be careful in observing the Sabbatical years". The general rule we know is that good things are greater than disastrous things. If the sin of desecrating the Sabbatical years causes the exile of Israel, then all the more so we see that the merit of observing the Seventh Year according to the laws thereof will help us to be worthy to return to the Land in the future. This is what is hinted to by the Scripture "when you come into the Land that I give you", meaning when Israel returns to the Land in the future it will be by God's Hand alone, and this will happen only

in the merit of "and the Land shall rest a Sabbath unto the Lord". When we observe the commandment of the Sabbatical correctly today, it gives us the merit that we will stand to inherit the Holy Land (in the future after the Messiah comes).
(Divrei Yoel)

PARSHAS BECHUKOSAI

"And I will give peace in the Land"

Rashi explains that "you might say, 'we have food and drinks, but if there is no peace we have nothing', thus after all of these blessings, God says 'And I will give peace in the Land'." We can explain this based on the known question of the commentators how the Children of Israel left Egypt before the proper time, and they answer either 1.) that the Exile was counted from the time of Isaac's birth or 2.) that the difficulty of the bondage counted in place of the extra years, or 3.) that the future exiles made up for the extra years. However, this brings a question, because we know that we were exiled from our Land because of our sins, and if we did not sin, we would not have been exiled. If this is so, how could we have fulfilled the decree of four hundred years of exile? The Divrei Chaim answers that if the Children of Israel were worthy, they would have caused that in Heaven they would have accepted one of the other answers. Since they were not worthy, their sin caused the decision to be that the answer is that the other exiles make up the years. It is cited in the Talmud that it would have been proper if Jacob had gone down to Egypt in iron chains like a captive exile. However, he was only exiled in an honorable fashion because he did not have what to eat. This shows that a decree of exile can be fulfilled either by going captive in iron chains or through "and there was a difficult famine in the Land". And now the Children of Israel knew that they did not fulfill the decreed time of exile in Egypt, and that they would need to make it up later. If this is so, once they were promised "and I will give you your rain in its proper time", then it showed that the only way they would go into exile would be through the difficult suffering of being brought captive in iron chains. This is what it says "maybe you will say 'we have what to eat and drink, but if there is no peace there is nothing'." This means that they understood that they would

need to go into exile through war. Thus, Scripture says after all of this, meaning after all of the blessings in this passage are fulfilled of "if you walk in my statues" it says "I will give you peace" because then it will be decided in Heaven (how we will have paid for those other years) according to the other answers.
(Divrei Yoel)

NUMBERS/BEMIDBAR

PARSHAS BEMIDBAR

"Lift up the heads of the Children of Israel"

The Midrash connects this to the verse "He has not done so for any nation, and He lifts up the pride of His People" (Psalms). Why do we make a census? To fulfill the verse "He has not done so for any nation", and what has He done, "and He lifts up the pride of His People". We can understand this according to the words of the Commentators who explain the reason why God commanded to count the Children of Israel was in order to push away the claims of the gentile nations that they are the majority of the world, thus the Jews are nullified being "the least of all the peoples", thus Israel should be drawn into idolatry like the majority. That is why God commanded to count the Israelites, because then they would become something counted (*davar shebeminyan*), which does not become nullified in a majority, and no nullification can come to them (according to Jewish law, a counted item is not nullified). This is the meaning of the Midrash "why does it say 'lift up the heads of the children of Israel'?" Meaning "why count the Israelites?" in order to fulfill what is written "and He has not done so for any nation", because through this they will be separated from every nation and language, "and He lifts up the pride of His People" to make them a treasured People (Am Segulah). Then the nations will not be able to come with a complaint as to why we are separated from them, because a counted item is not nullified by a majority. (Divrei Yoel)

PARSHAS NASO

"Lift up the heads of the sons of Gershon, they as well, according to the houses of their patriarchs, according to their families"

It seems that we can explain this based on what is taught in the holy book "Ohev Yisrael" teaching that all of the souls of Israel for all times were included in the holy Patriarchs, for they are the roots from which all of the branches spread. When one of our holy Patriarchs performed a mitzvah, a tremendous benefit sprouted from it to the future generations after them until the end of time, because every Israelite soul was included within the holy Patriarchs. Thus, when one of the holy Patriarchs fulfilled a mitzvah, then all of the Jewish souls included within them from their roots also performed the mitzvah with them. Also, this mitzvah forged a path for future generations to perform the mitzvos properly, because the door was already opened for them to do so from the days of our Patriarch Abraham, peace be upon him.

We can also add to this what is taught in the sacred literature of Hasidism and Kabbalah, that when one sees that his soul constantly and strongly desires to perform a particular mitzvah, and his heart is drawn after that mitzvah, to be worthy to fulfill it all of the time, then one can know that the main reason his soul came into the world was for the sake of that Mitzvah. Then that Mitzvah is from the soul-root to which this particular mitzvah is more closely related.

According to these two concepts, we can answer the question of the Kli Yakar, of blessed memory, who asked why the more sacred tasks, such as carrying the Ark of the Covenant, was not given to the sons of Gershon, seeing that Gershon was the first born of his family. The answer is that all of this is dependent upon the soul roots that one has as to why he came into the world. If this is the case, then this Divine Service is connected to the soul-roots of the sons of Kehath, thus it would not be taken from them. This is why it says "lift up the heads of the sons of Gershon", to lift up and appoint the sons of Gershon to have the appointment of guarding the Temple, and not to feel that this is inferior to the appointment of the sons of Kehath in any way, to think that the Kehathites are somehow superior in their different type of service. This is why it says "they as well", meaning that the sons of Gershon are also appointed to their guardianship position according to their soul-root they are connected to this service specifically. Also, it ends "according to the houses of their Patriarchs, according to their families" meaning that that part of their soul included in the souls of the holy Patriarchs.

(Divrei Yoel)

"May the Lord bless you and keep you"

The Midrash teaches "may the Lord bless you" with Talmud (i.e., with study of Torah), "and keep you" that your merits should be written down. We might want to explain this based on the teaching of the Talmud that "The early pious men would wait for an hour, pray for an hour, and wait for an hour (preparing for prayer through meditation before and after the prayer). Since they were busy in prayer for nine hours a day, how was their Torah kept and how was their work done? However, since they were pious men, their Torah was guarded and their work was blessed." The Yismach Moshe in Parshas Chayeh Sarah explains that "everything that God gives as a reward for a person's mitzvah observance comes from God's Loving Kindness and Grace, because God gave us the power in the first place to do the mitzvah, and He also finishes it for us as well. However, His Kindness is abundant upon us that He allows us to think as if the entire mitzvah was accomplished through human effort. However, according to this, one may be worried that not every time is the same, and there are times when the attributes of Strict Justice are controlling the world. However, in God's abundant Kindness, as soon as a person performs a mitzvah it is already written down in a book that he had done it, and it is recorded that he is owed a reward for this mitzvah, as it is written 'and all of your deeds are written in a book', and one who would complain about this to a court of law would not be able to accomplish anything against this that is written." This is the meaning of "May the Lord bless you" with Talmud, that He should bless the wellsprings of your Torah study in order to understand the blessings of God in the Holy Torah, as the Torah blesses a person. However, since this is only from the side of God's Loving Kindness, it is possible that the attributes of Strict Justice would not agree to this and a person would not receive his reward.

This is why it says "and guard you" that your merits should be written. Because the merit of the Torah is written in a book and your merits are recorded. Thus, there is nothing to worry about because once a Court of Law has decided something there is no way to change it, and the reward is coming to you according to strict law.

(Divrei Yoel)

PARSHAS BEHAALOSECHA

"When you raise up the lights across the face of the Menorah to illuminate the seven lamps"

We could say, according to what is cited in the Midrash, that the seven branches of the Menorah correspond to the seven days of the week. The Sages teach that the three days before the Sabbath belong to the coming Sabbath, and that the three days after the Sabbath belong to the previous Sabbath. If that is the case, then we find that the middle lamp hints to the Sabbath day, which is the middle day between the three days before the Sabbath and the three days after the Sabbath. It is

known that the influence of holiness that rests upon a person depends upon someone preparing his deeds during the week. This is why it says "when you raise up the lights" means to raise up the weekdays, which correspond to the lamps of the Menorah, up to holiness. This means that your intentions should be "across the face of the Menorah to illuminate the seven lamps" which means the middle lamp that hints to the Sabbath. This means that through illuminating into the days of the week you will be worthy to the blessings on the Sabbath day, because it is dependent upon that.
(Divrei Yoel)

PARSHAS SHLACH

"And Moses called Hosea the son of Nun 'Joshua'."

It is cited in Targum Jonathan that "when Moses saw the humility of Hosea, he called him 'Joshua'."

We can explain this based on how it is known that the Spies had some ulterior motive in their mission, inasmuch as they had leadership roles in the desert, and once they came into the Land of Israel they would no longer be able to have their positions. This brought them into this folly to bring back a bad report. The opposite was the case with Joshua. In the desert, he was not yet recognized as a leader in Israel, but in the Land of Israel he was destined to be the leader. However, Joshua also would have had an ulterior motive to bring a bad report as the other spies did. Since he was so humble, he ran away from honor and did not wish to be the leader. Therefore, he also would have had some reason why he would desire for the Israelites to remain in the desert, so he would not become the leader. However, there is a difference between them, as the ulterior motive of the ten spies came from arrogance. Our Sages teach that God says of an arrogant person that "I and he cannot dwell in one place", thus they were not worthy to Divine Providence to save them from sin, because God's blessing had no place to rest in their court. The opposite was so with Joshua. His ulterior motive was the opposite of the other spies, as he was running away from honor. Thus, he was worthy to Divine Providence to guide him on the True Path and to save him from sin.

This is the meaning of the Targum Jonathan, "when Moses saw the humility of Hosea, he called him 'Joshua'", as he saw Joshua's great humility, and understood that this could have caused him to err. Thus, Moses prayed for Joshua, saying "may God save you from the advice of the spies" (the Yud and Hei from God's Name, which was added to Joshua's name). Moses understood that God would save Joshua from the advice of the spies, because Joshua had perfected the attribute of humility.
(Divrei Yoel)

PARSHAS KORACH

"And Korah took"

The Midrash teaches that Korah saw the passage of the Torah teaching about the Red Heifer, and saw a way to disagree with Moses.

It is further written "And they stood up before Moses... men of Name". The term is usually rendered "men of renown", but the Yalkut teaches that the term means "men who know God's Explicit Name". Perhaps we could explain that Moses also knew God's Explicit Name, as the Yalkut teaches on the verse in Exodus "and My Name, HASHEM, I did not make known to them", means that God did not explain the Explicit Name to the Patriarch, but He did reveal it to Moses, as Moses was set to redeem Israel. Thus, the Name was revealed to him so he could be successful. God told him "In This World, I only revealed the Name to certain individuals. However, in the Next World, I will make My Name known to all Israel". See there in the Yalkut.

We see from here that it is a necessity of the Redemption to have the Explicit Name to be known. It is known that Korah had an opinion to bring near the Final Redemption, which will eventually come in the future. For this, he needed the Explicit Name of God. That is why Korah took "Men of Name" with him, meaning men who knew God's Explicit Name, thus he would be able to draw the Final Redemption near. However, the

Arizal writes that only those who are purified with the ashes of the Red Heifer are permitted to use the Holy Name. Thus, it did not help them any if they only knew the Name, since they would not be able to utilize the Name in a state of impurity. However, once they saw that Moses would teach the Bible Passage of the Red Heifer, they saw a way to purify those who were defiled, through the ashes of the Red Heifer. Thus, he then raised his heart to contradict Moses, with the help of "Men of Name", who knew the Explicit Name of God. (Divrei Yoel)

PARSHAS CHUKAS

"And take for you a red heifer"

The Midrash teaches that we learn from here "that a red heifer may be accepted from a gentile, and this is what is written "all of the nations are like nothing before Him, and as zero and emptiness are the considered to Him" (Isaiah 40:17)."

One might say that before we can explain this that we should mention what is written in the

"Mikdash Melech", that the entire concept of a Red Heifer is one of specific Divine Providence, that one should find a perfectly red cow that does not have even two white hairs, etc. This makes the issue even more difficult to understand, because it begs us to ask why would God do such a thing to make it that such a cow (needed for such an important and rare mitzvah) should only be found in the property of a heathen?

We can understand this based on how the Midrash expounded this entire passage to pertain to the nations of the world. "Heifer" refers to Egypt. "Red" refers to Babylonia. "Perfect" refers to Medea. "And you shall slaughter it in his presence" (refers to Edom), as it is written "and a sacrifice to the LORD in Botzrah" (Isaiah 34:6). "And you shall burn the heifer before his eyes" as it is written "and it will be given to the burning fire" (Daniel 7:11). This teaches that by the power of the Red Heifer will come the humbling of the nations.

It is cited in the Talmud (Sanhedrin 39b) on the verse "The vision of Obadiah, thus says the LORD God to Edom" (Obadiah 1:1), asking why Obadiah was distinguished to prophecy to Edom?

The Talmud answers that Obadiah was a convert of Edomite descent. This is meaning of the popular saying that "from itself comes the ax". Rashi explains this saying to mean that "from the forest itself comes the handle for the ax to chop down the forest." Thus, was Obadiah to Edom. This is how we can understand how Divine Providence can provide that a Red Heifer would be found to be received from a gentile. This is because the Red Heifer represents the humbling of the nations. This humbling power is stronger if it comes from the very nation set to be humbled. This is why the Midrash continues to say that this is the meaning of the Scripture "and all of the nations are as nothing before Him", because this is the purpose of the Red Heifer, that all of the nations should be as nothing before Him, in order that all of the Wicked Kingdoms should speedily be destroyed (and peace will reign on Earth). (Divrei Yoel)

PARSHAS BALAK

"And Balak saw"

It is cited in the Baal HaTurim that "Balak saw" that the sun stood still in the sky for Moses during the war with Sihon. We could explain this based on what the Talmud (Brachos 7a) teaches concerning the verse "and he knows the knowledge of the Most High", that Balaam knew the precise moment when God is angry each day. "And when is He angry? Abaye says, 'in one moment of those first three hours of the day...'." Tosafos writes that this is speaking of the "time close to when the sun's rays begin to shine, when the kings of the East and the West put on their crowns and bow worship the sun, immediately God is angry."

According to this, we can explain that when Moses caused the sun to stand still, it caused a confusion in the time schedule of those kings. It is possible that in the morning, when the sun was scheduled to shine, the order of the rotation was interrupted, thus the kings did not know when to make their pagan worship. We see that this nullified God's anger, because the kings did not offer their worship to the sun. This is what is meant when it says that Balak saw that our teacher Moses was able to cause the sun to stand still, because that would change the moment of God's anger, and interrupt his entire plan to have Balaam curse the Israelites at that moment.

(Divrei Yoel)

"And Moab was bothered by the Children of Israel"

Rashi explains that they were bothered by their very life. We can explain this based on what is taught in the holy book Agra D'Kallah, (Parshas Lech Lecha), on the verse "And I will establish my covenant with Isaac", to which the Midrash teaches "Rabbi Abba said that from here you can learn that if the son of the maidservant is blessed, then all the more so the son of the mistress of the house. By Ishmael is it written 'behold, I have blessed him and I will increase him', thus we can say all the more so 'I will establish my covenant with Isaac'." Until here are the words of the Midrash. We have already quoted the Agra D'Kallah's words many times here, and a brief summary of his words are that if, God forbid, the

Jewish people are not worthy of their own accord, they will be saved by the power of this "all the more so" argument, that can be expounded from the Torah, to say that the Jewish people are owed kindness and goodness from God. This can be argued "all the more so" from the success and greatness of Ishmael. See there.

It is possible that this is the intent behind the words "And Moab was bothered", which Rashi explains "bothered by their very lives" "because of the Children of Israel", because through their lives they will draw down kindness and goodness to the Jewish people through this "all the more so" argument, (because if the heathens are successful, all the more so the Jews should be). But because of the tremendous wickedness of the Moabites, they are disgusted and repulsed by their very own lives, because they do not want their own lives to cause goodness to sprout for the Jewish people. (Divrei Yoel)

PARSHAS PINCHAS

"When he was zealous for the sake of My zeal"

It is cited in the Midrash that "he took his pay with justice". We can explain this in accordance with what is taught in the holy book Noam Elimelech, to explain the Scripture "when he was zealous for the sake of My zeal... and I did not destroy the Children of Israel", that when there is judgment below, there is no judgment Above, this is the meaning of "he was zealous for My zeal, and I did not destroy them", because through Phineas executing judgment upon them below, "I did not destroy them", because he caused an awakening of God's tremendous Mercy upon them. Until here are the words of the Noam Elimelech.

This is how we can explain the words of the Midrash that "he took his payment with justice", that when the attribute of strict justice is strong in the world, may God save us in His Mercy, it is very difficult for one to receive his just rewards, because there is a prosecutor pushing back through strict judgement. But, since Phineas made executed the judgement himself, he awoke the attribute of Mercy in the world, since "when there is judgment below there is no judgment Above". Thus, even the powers of justice agreed that Phineas had earned his reward. This is what is meant by "he took his payment with justice", that even the attribute of strict justice gave Phineas his reward.

(Divrei Yoel)

"May the Lord, the God of the spirits of all flesh, appoint a man over the congregation who will go forth before them and come in before them."

We can explain this based on the words of the Holy Rebbe from Ropshitz, who commented on that which is cited in the Midrash that "God showed Moses each generation and its preachers, each generation and its judges". The Ropshitzer Rebbe pointed out that it does not say that He showed him "the preacher and then his generation", because if God had shown him the preachers, righteous people, and judges of this generation, he would have been very surprised. Thus, Moses was first shown the generation, so we could understand that each generation has their preachers, judges, and righteous people based on the deeds of that generation, as they are worthy for their generation. Until here is the teaching of Rabbi Naftali Tzvi of Ropshitz.

This teaching was said about the level of the generation of the Ropshitzer (when leaders lead), however in our generation there is no question why the generation was shown before the leaders. Due to our abundant sins, it is the people of the generation themselves who are the leaders, because the leaders of this generation lead based on the will of the people of the generation. Thus it makes sense in this generation to show the people of the generation first, and then to show the preachers and leaders. This is why Moses specifically prayed that God should appoint a man over them who will specifically go out "before them and who is come in before them", and that the leader should not operate based on the will of the people of the generation, but rather that he should truly lead the generation.
(Divrei Yoel)

PARSHAS MATTOS

"Take the revenge of the Children of Israel against the Midianites"

First, we have to examine why the soldiers made the mistake of keeping the females of Midian alive. The soldiers loved Moses immensely, and since they knew that his death was dependent upon the revenge against Midian, they tried to make sure that the revenge would be incomplete, as they thought that this would delay the death of Moses that was depending upon the revenge against Midian. When Moses saw that such lofty righteous men made such a mistake, he assumed that it must be God's Will as well that the revenge against Midian should be incomplete, in order to delay his death so he could live longer and still have time to pray more so he would be authorized to enter the Holy Land. However, there was a vow and an oath from God that Moses would not enter the Holy Land, as Rashi writes that after the wars of Sihon and Og, Moses thought that perhaps he was released from the vow. We find that in order to nullify the decree, he needed to follow the commandments of the release of vows. This is what we find in the Talmud, Tractate Brachos,

concerning the Scripture "And Moses entreated God" to which Rava said that he sought to be released from His vow. We need to say that this means that Moses thought that God would release him from His vow, and authorize him to enter the Holy Land. Through this, he came to this mistake in the revenge against Midian, which is why the paragraph concerning the revenge against Midian is next to the paragraph teaching the laws of vows.
(Divrei Yoel)

PARSHAS MASEI

"And Moses wrote their goings out according to their travels"

One could explain this by first quoting the words of the Zera Kodesh, that in every stage of their travels in the desert, there was another klipah (impure shell) resting there. When the Israelites rested in each of those places, they made tikunim (spiritual rectifications) in each place, according to the needs of that place, to nullify the klipah that existed in that place. The names of the Klipos and the types of Tikunim the Israelites did in each of those places are hinted to by the names of each stage. Until here are the words of the Zera Kodesh.

This is what is hinted to by the words of the Scripture "And Moses wrote their goings out (or "takings out") according to their travels", that the concepts of the sparks of holiness that they "took out" were all written down by Moses and hinted to by the names of the stages. Also, it is written "and these are their travels according to their taking out", to mean that the purpose of these travels was "their taking out", meaning to "take out" the sparks of holiness through their service of God through Torah and Mitzvos, and sanctification in holiness.

(Divrei Yoel)

DEUTERONOMY/DEVARIM

PARSHAS DEVARIM

"These are the words which Moses spoke to all of Israel"

We can understand this based on the words of the holy Rebbe from Ropshitz, zy"a, that no prosecution of sin can come before the Throne of Glory because of its holiness. And it is said in the books of Mussar (ethical teachings) that in the place where a sin in mentioned, that world is immersed in many immersions (like in a mikvah). Thus, we can be sure that no sin can actually come before God, but rather only the holy root to be found within the sin, such as the fact that through sin one can come to repent, as we know that penitents are considered to be extremely great people. Thus, the prosecution that is permitted to enter into God's Presence is only that so-and-so did such a deed that can be fixed with such-and-such a type of repentance. Until here are his words.

Through this, we can comment upon the first verse in Deuteronomy, "These are the words", as this is said in the same sense of "this is the word", and the Shechinah speaks through the throat of Moses. Thus, the sins are not mentioned openly before God, but rather are only mentioned in the form of hints, and the hints are only to the roots that the sins have in holiness, because we repented for these sins. This is what is written in the Targum Jonathan "and Di Zahab..." is translated as "and they atoned for the Golden Calf".

(Divrei Yoel)

"These are the words"

It seems to me that to answer the question of the commentators as to why Moses only hints to the sins of Israel here, while in later portions he mentions them openly. If he hides them for the sake of their honor, why is he not worried about their honor there as well? We can explain this based on the holy words of the Kedushas Levi, zt"l, (Parshas Haazinu) to explain the words of our Sages, z"l, on the verse (about the feast of Sukkos) "and you shall take for yourself on the first day", to which they ask "is this the first day? Is it not the fifteenth day of the month? Rather it is the first day of the counting of sins". His teaching can be summarized by the known teaching of our Sages that through Repentance from fear, intentional sins are transformed into unintentional sins. On the other hand, through Repentance from love, intentional sins are transformed into merits. Thus, on this festival, where we come to be sheltered in the Shadow of God, through the mitzvos and good deeds from love of God, then we count all of our sins in order to know how many will be turned into mitzvos. However, until Sukkos we are serving through fear, thus we do not count the sins at all, because they are still counted as unintentional sins. This is the meaning of "the first day of counting sins". See there in the Kedushas Levi to examine the matter further.

We already explained above that this rebuke was not given by Moses in order to separate them from a sin that they were actively engaging in, because the Israelites were already cleansed from these sins and had them atoned for. However, Moses was rebuking them in order to raise them to a higher level of repentance, which is from love. The Israelites accepted his rebuke, as is taught in the Midrash Rabbah, that God told Moses, "now that Israel has accepted the rebuke, you need to bless them", and immediately Moses turned around and blessed them. This is why in the first verse of Deuteronomy, the sins are only hinted to, because before they repented out of love, the sins had not yet entered the counting of merits, thus it was good to conceal them. Even though they had already been turned as if they were accidental, accidents are still not considered as a source of honor to Israel to mention them, thus they were only mentioned here in the form of a hint. However, after they repented out of love and the sins became merits, from then on, they were mentioned openly, as this is a source of honor. (Divrei Yoel)

PARSHAS VAES'CHANAN

"Please pass me over so I will see the good land"

It is cited in the Midrash "if you want 'please pass me over' to be fulfilled, then 'please forgive' will be nullified. If you want 'please forgive' to be fulfilled, then 'please pass me over' will be nullified." It is understood based on what is brought in Pirkei D'Rabbi Eliezer that every year at the time when the Israelites sinned with the daughters of Moab, at that very place and time, Peor goes up above to prosecute Israel and to recall their sin. When he sees the grave of Moses, he is quieted and returns. This means that it was necessary to bury Moses outside the Holy Land facing Beth Peor, in order to atone for the sin of worshipping Peor. This is what is written in the holy Ohr HaChaim, "and we will sit in the valley, across from Beth Peor" as the term "sitting" refers to holding back for all time. Thus Moses hinted to the reason for his burial to be facing Beth Peor, which is that it serves to keep prosecution from raising its head against Israel. Until here are the words of the Holy Ohr HaChaim.

Rashi says on the verse "for I will die in this land, as I will not pass over the Jordan River" that it means that even the bones of Moses will not pass over the river. Thus, we see that it seems that Moses' request to pass over the river was only that he should be buried in the Holy Land. This is why God answered him this word, because if He would fulfill the request of "please allow me to pass", with Moses being buried in the Holy Land, then the request of "please forgive the sin" would be nullified, because if he were not buried facing Beth Peor, then there would be an opportunity for prosecution every year. Thus, if you wish to have the request of "please forgive" be fulfilled, to remove the prosecution from the sin of Peor, then you need to nullify the request of "please allow me to pass over the river", in order to be buried facing Beth Peor for the reason mentioned. (Divrei Yoel)

PARSHAS EKEV

"Not because of your righteousness nor the uprightness of your heart do you come to inherit the Land, but because of the wickedness of these nations"

We can understand this based on the words of the Midrash on the verse "and I have listened to you concerning Ishmael... and My covenant I will fulfill in Isaac" as we can learn concerning the son of the matriarch from the son of the maidservant. "I have blessed him", this is Ishmael, all the more so "and My covenant I will fulfill in Isaac."

The Agra D'Kallah asks why do we need this argument of "all the more so"? God already promised the covenant to Isaac. The answer is that God's promise to Abraham concerning Isaac was contingent upon his faithfulness to the Laws of the Torah. However, once we see that God heard Abraham concerning Ishmael, it shows that the blessing will come even without any merit. Through this will kindness and goodness come to the seed of Isaac even if, God forbid, they have no merit. Then they will be saved by the "all the more so" argument that we can make from the success and greatness of Ishmael. And in these End Times, if we have no merit or righteousness, God forbid, we can still argue that we have hope to be saved through the power of this "all the more so" argument. Until here is the teaching of the Agra D'Kallah.

Rashi writes in Tractate Sotah that the Children of Israel are paid back quickly in this world, and they are scrutinized closely. This is what is said, "Not because of your righteousness or the uprightness of your heart". Even though the generation of the desert were righteous people, it was still possible for the attributes of strict justice to prosecute them, inasmuch as the attributes of

strict justice scrutinize Israel closely. However, "because of the wickedness of these nations" we are blessed, because the nations of the world receive blessing even if they are wicked, thus we also deserve blessings by virtue of the justice of an argument of "all the more so", because if God blesses those who violate His Will, then those who keep His Will all the more so! This is what is written "you shall be blessed from all nations" (usually interpreted that Israel is blessed more than all nations, but here interpreted that the blessings come from the nations), which means that the blessings will come to you from the power of the nations. Since they stand in their greatness and peace, thus we also deserve the same blessing from the power of an argument of "all the more so".
(Divrei Yoel)

PARSHAS RE'EH

"See that I have placed before you today a blessing and a curse"

We can explain this based on what my revered father, zt"l wrote in Kedushas Yom Tov, to explain the teaching of the Talmud in Tractate Shabbos concerning the Chanukah Candles, as Beis Shammai taught to start with eight candles on the first night and to subtract each night down to one, while Beis Hillel taught to start with one candle on the first night and add each night up to eight. He taught that all of our service to God has the goal of widening the borders of holiness and bringing the downfall of the sitra achra (other side - i.e. side of evil) and to subdue it. One depends upon the other, as there is a reaction between the two sides, as nature abhors a vacuum, thus when one rises the other falls. Thus Beis Shammai, who comes from the side of gevurah (strength or restraint - to be introverted) held to subtract each night, which indicated the destruction of the klippah (shell, i.e. power of impurity) which would automatically lead to an increase in holiness. And Beis Hillel, who comes from the side of chesed (kindness or love - to be extroverted) held to add each night, meaning if we do good deeds we will increase the power of holiness, which will automatically decrease the impurity. Until here are the teachings of the Kedushas Yom Tov.

It is known that the halachah (decided law) follows Beis Hillel against Beis Shammai. Thus, the main thing is to draw down the blessing to Israel, which means to strengthen the power of holiness. The curses will then fall upon the heads of our enemies through this, and their power will be weakened. This is the intention of the scripture, "See I have set before you today a blessing and a curse", blessing refers to raising the power of holiness, and curse refers to lowering the power of impurity. When the Jews involve themselves in the study of Torah and in performing mitzvos, we lift up the power of holiness and subdue the power of impurity, for when this rises that falls. Thus, Scripture mentions the blessing before the curse, because we must focus on the positive aspect of the blessing, which will automatically send the curse to the sitra achra.
(Divrei Yoel)

PARSHAS SHOFTIM

"Lest he deviate from the commandment to the right or the left"

One could say that this hints to what our Sages taught on the Scriptural verse "And all the host of heaven stand upon Him from His right and from His left" (I Kings 22:19 and II Chronicles 18:18). The Sages ask whether there is a "left hand" to Heaven? Does it not say "the Right Hand of the Lord is exalted; the Right Hand of the Lord does valor" (Psalm 118)? The meaning is that some (of the angels mentioned) push things to the right and some push things to the left. Those who are on the right side try to find merit and those who are on the left side try to find fault.

A Jewish king and other Jewish leaders need to have both of these attributes. They need to rebuke the people and declare their faults before them (i.e. in public discourse), in order not to give them false flattery. However, in regard to Heaven (i.e. in prayer), they need to find merits in Israel. This is as is stated in the Midrash that God said to

Moses "it is as if you have rebuked Me for the Children of Israel and you have rebuked the Children of Israel for Me. You said to Israel 'you have sinned before God', and to God you have said 'why, oh Lord, do You have such anger to Your People?'."

Wicked leaders do the opposite. They flatter the people falsely and declare their merits in their presence, and do not rebuke them. This brings prosecution against them in Heaven (because do they really deserve this praise?). This is the statement of the Scripture, "lest he turn from the commandment to the right or to the left." The Jewish king is commanded concerning these two things, right and left, to declare merits of the people to Heaven and to rebuke the people to their face. But do not reverse the order. If he does so, he will reign for many days.
(Divrei Yoel)

PARSHAS KI SEITZEI

"When a man has two wives, one beloved and one hated."

The Midrash teaches that "beloved" refers to the gentiles, as God shows favoritism to them. "Hated" refers to the Jewish people, as God hides His Face from them. "On the day of dividing inheritance" refers to the future time. "You cannot give the birthright to the beloved son" but rather He will have to give the birthright to "My firstborn son, Israel". Until here are the words of the Midrash.

It is difficult to understand how the Midrash could call the Jewish people "hated". In order to understand this, we have to quote my comments on the verse "and the LORD saw that Leah was hated". The Talmud asks "Was she actually hated? Rather, God saw that she hated the deeds of Esau, so God opened her womb". Until here are the words of the Talmud.

It seems that our Sages were changing the meaning of this verse, as the simple meaning was that Leah herself was hated, however the Sages expounded that she hated someone else. Even according to the simple meaning of the Scripture that others hated her, it is not an insult to her, because she hated the deeds of Esau, which is what caused people to hate her. Thus, since this was the reason for others hating her, this was not an insult to her but rather a praise to her.

This is the meaning of the Midrash that "a beloved one" means the gentiles, meaning that they are beloved in this world, but not that God loves them. The Midrash only says that God shows them favor; meaning that by the way things look in the eyes of the world everything is good for the gentiles. However, the Jews are hated in this world, because all the nations hate the Jews. The reason for this is because the Jewish people hate the ways of Esau, thus the gentiles hate them. This is a praise to the Jewish people. The Midrash does not say that God hates them, God forbid, but rather that He hides His Face from them, meaning that they do not live in peace in this world and they are hated in the eyes of the gentile nations. However, in Heaven, just the opposite is the case. Since the Jewish people hate the ways of Esau, they are beloved before God, and the heathens are hated before God.
(Divrei Yoel)

PARSHAS KI SAVO

"I have not passed over from your commandments and I have not forgotten"

It seems that one could understand this that it would seem that it is just the opposite, he did good in this that he did not forget to fulfill the command of God. We could explain this based on the words of the Holy Rebbe from Nikolsburg, to explain the words from the High Holiday Liturgy "for You remember all forgotten things forever" to mean that if a person sins before God, but he remembers his sin constantly to regret it and to repent for it, then God forgets about it and erases the sin. However, if a person forgets about his sins after he commits it, then God remembers the sin and it is imprinted in the Book of Remembrances. It is just the opposite with a mitzvah. If one performs a mitzvah and then forgets about it, and considers it as if he never did the mitzvah, meaning he recognizes his failings and realizes that he falls short of fulfilling God's commandments properly, then God appreciates the mitzvah and remembers it. However, if a person sees his path as being upright in his own eyes, and after he performed the mitzvah he imagines that he fulfilled his obligation properly, and he lifts up his heart in pride, never forgetting that he fulfilled God's Will, then this mitzvah does not ascend Above, and it is as if God forgot about it. This is the intent in the words of the Liturgy "for You remember the forgotten things forever", that God only "remembers" the things that people forget about. Until here is the teaching of Rebbe Shmelke from Nikolsburg, zya.

This is what a person confesses when he brings his first fruits to the Temple, "I have not passed from Your commandments", however he recognizes his failure inasmuch as "and I have not forgotten", meaning when a person fulfills a mitzvah he has to forget that he fulfilled it, so he should not become arrogant because of it. Thus, he has to confess his sin of arrogance.

(Divrei Yoel)

PARSHAS NITZAVIM

"That the watered be included with the dry" (Deuteronomy 29:18)

Rashi explains that this means that God will add punishment for the unintentional sins, and include them with the intentional sins, and have everything paid for from him. "Watered" means that which is unintentional and accidental, without knowledge or intent, and "dry" means intentional sins done with full knowledge and intent out of lust.

It seems unfair to include unintentional transgressions together with the intentional ones, however this can be understood based on what is written "I will visit the sin of the fathers upon the children", to which the Talmud explains "if they continue following the ways of their parents". This means that a person can even be punished in several future reincarnations because of sins he committed in previous incarnations, if the wicked person holds onto his way. When it says "they are holding their parents' deeds" it is speaking of reincarnation (with "parent" being a metaphor for a previous incarnation). These sins that were done in previous incarnations are only blemishes upon the soul, however this present body did not commit this sin, only a different body with this soul. Thus, it is considered to be an unintentional sin with regard to this body. This is why Scripture calls this "watered", because this person did not thirst to commit this sin, and it was committed without his intent or will, thus it is impossible for him to be punished for this sin, as it is considered accidental by him. However, if one holds on to his ancestors' deeds, and adds to his record of intentional sins in this reincarnation, then he is called "thirsty", meaning that he commits this sin with full lust and desire out of the crookedness of his own heart. Then God, may He be Blessed, will punish the person even for the previous sins, and include them with these.

(Divrei Yoel)

PARSHAS VAYELECH

"And Moses went and he spoke these words to all of Israel"

It seems that we can explain this based on the words of the Holy Rebbe, the Rebbe Reb Shmelke from Nikolsburg, zt"l, on the verse "Go children, listen to me, I will teach you the fear of the LORD" (Psalm 34). He taught that when people hear words of rebuke from a Sage delivering a sermon, it awakens their heart to repent. But when they leave the synagogue and go to their houses, they forget the entire subject of the sermon, and return to their habits. This is what the Scripture warns by saying "go children", meaning when you go away from me, then you shall "listen to me" as to what is "the fear of the LORD that I teach you", and you will not return to your wicked deeds that you have been habituated into doing until now. This is a summary of his teaching.

This is how my holy grandfather, zt"l, the Yetev Lev, explained that which is cited in the Midrash Rabbah on Parshas Ki Savo (ch. 10), that God said to Moses "you asked 'please allow me pass (over the Jordan River)', and you also asked 'please forgive'. If there is 'please allow me to pass' then there is no place here for 'please forgive'... etc."

From the first day of the month of Elul until after Hoshana Rabbah, there are 51 days of penitence (51 being the Gematria of "na" or "please"). If after these days, one says "51 (na/please) days of penitence have 'passed' (similar to the words "please allow me to pass"), so now I can return to my original ways, then there is no place here for 'please forgive'." This is the meaning of "if 'na' (51) has passed", meaning one says the 51 days have passed so now "back to normal" then there is no place here for "please forgive", as one does not deserve forgiveness if he does not try to improve his ways. This is a summary of his teaching.

Moses just told the Israelites words of rebuke. He told them words that pierce the heart and go down into the depth of the gut. This was so there should remain an impression upon them, so that even after they leave him the imprint is recognizable. Then it is considered as if Moses was still standing over them and speaking to them. Through this, they would always have thoughts of repentance and improve their deeds. This is the meaning of the verse, and "and Moses went", meaning that even when Moses went away from them to his house, he was still speaking to them "these words".

(Divrei Yoel)

"And they will say on that day: Are not these evils come upon us because God is not among us?" (Deuteronomy 31:17)

And I said to explain the intent of the Scripture to be that in the End Days, because of the great tribulations that will come with the birth pangs of the Messiah, many Jews will say that "God is not with us", meaning that God has removed His Providence from upon us, God forbid. However, the truth will not be so; rather God is with us and among us at every time and in every situation. We have to know that His Presence, may He be Blessed, is found among us always, but sometimes He is greatly hidden. This is the intent of the Scripture "and they will say in that day: Are not these evils come upon us because God is not among us?", that because of the overwhelming impact of these troubles, it will appear, God forbid, that "the Lord has abandoned the Land", and that "God is not among us". However, the truth is not so. Rather it is "and I will surely hide My Face", meaning that God is always with us, only sometimes He is hidden.

(Divrei Yoel: Rosh Hashanah p. 66)

"When I was still alive, you were already rebellious with the LORD" (Deuteronomy 31:27)

It seems that it should have said "rebellious against the LORD", what is the meaning of "rebellious with the LORD"? We can understand this based on how the Noam Megadim explained the words of our Sages that "Jerusalem was only destroyed when they based their own words on the Torah law", which means that even when they did things that were not good they hung it upon the Holy Torah, as if to say that the Torah commands this improper thing. This came about through improper and untrue interpretations of the Torah. Until here is a summary of his teaching.

We can similarly say that the dispute that Korah and his followers made against Moses and against his prophecy from God's Mouth was also based on proofs that they took from words of Torah, that they perverted the ways of the Torah into their own opinions and desires. This is what Moses meant when he said "when I still lived, you were rebellious 'with' the LORD", and he did not say "against the LORD", meaning that they used God's own Words to rebel against His Will, by turning His Word around. Thus, Moses felt it would be even worse after his death, for who would be around to rebuke them and to demonstrate their mistakes? Moses was the source through which God gave us the Torah, and despite that, the Torah's teachings were already perverted in his own days. Thus, Moses was worried as to what would happen after his death. (Divrei Yoel)

PARSHAS HAAZINU

"Hear O Heaven and I will speak. Listen, Earth, to the words of my mouth"

One would ask why does the tense change from the future tense to the present tense. "I will speak" is in the future tense. "The words of my mouth" is in the present tense. Also, "I will speak" refers to a tough type of speech (dibbur). "The words of my mouth" is a soft type of speech (amirah).

The Midrash Yalkut explains "Hear o Heavens" is used because the Torah was given from Heaven, as it is said "you have seen that the LORD speaks to you from Heaven". "And listen, Earth", the earth is where the Israelites were standing. And they said "All that the LORD says we will do and we will listen". Until here is the Midrash.

This seems to be a wonder, for who does not know that the Torah was given from heaven? Why does the Midrash have to tell us this here? Also, what is said here "listen, heaven"? The Torah was no longer in heaven at this point, as it is written "it is not in heaven".

The Midrash speaks of a Jew who had an ear ache and when to ask if it were permitted for him to seek healing on the Sabbath. The Sages taught that any case of a doubt of a danger to life overrides the Sabbath. If this ear ache could be considered a danger to life, then they could heal him on the Sabbath. The Rabbis said, "God said 'if you turn your ear to Torah', when you go to open a discourse with words of Torah, all desire to be near you." Where did Moses learn this? From "Hear, oh Heaven, and I will speak." Until here is the Midrash. We have to understand the legal connection that we find here.

We first need to examine the words of the Talmud (Yoma 85a), as to where we derive that a life-threatening situation overrides the Sabbath. While many interpretations are stated there in that passage of the Talmud, in the end "Rabbi Yehudah said in the name of Shmuel, 'if I were there, then my suggested opinion would be stronger than the others. It is simply that Scripture says 'and you shall live by them', thus we see that you should not die by them.' Rava said that he had a question to argue against all of the opinions, except for the opinion of Shmuel to which there is no question... Ravina said that one sharp pepper is better than a basket filled with bland pumpkins." Until here is the teaching of the Talmud. From this, we see that the main source for life threatening situations overriding the Sabbath is from the verse "and you shall live by them", for all of the other suggestions are questionable except for this one. See Rashi's commentary there, as well.

However, it would seem that there is also a question to this, from that which is cited in the Talmud (Chullin 142a), "It was taught: The house of Rabbi Yaakov says that every mitzvah, each of which has its reward on the side, has the Resurrection of the Dead dependant upon it as well. Concerning honoring father and mother it is written 'in order that you have a long life and in order that it should be good for you' (Deuteronomy 5). Concerning sending away the mother bird from her nest it is written 'in order that it should be good for you and you should have a long life'. It once occurred that someone was told by his father to go up on a ladder to get a bird's nest, and he went up and sent away the mother and took the babies. On his way down the ladder, he fell and died. Where is this one's longevity? Where is this one's good reward? Thus, the blessing of many days refers to the Next World, which is eternal. The blessing of goodness will come in the Next World, which is only good." Until here is the teaching of the Talmud. We see from here that when the Scripture promises long days, it is really talking about the Next World, which is eternal. If this is so, then we could say the same thing about the verse "and you shall live by them", to speak of eternal life. It is not necessary for the Sages to have expounded this verse to mean "you shall live by them" and not die by them, to refer to life in this world. Thus, we do not necessarily derive from here that a threat to life overrides the prohibitions of violating the Sabbath. This is similar to the teaching of the Holy Shlah, who taught that all of the prayers we say in our liturgy for the High Holidays, such as "remember us for life" and "inscribe us for life", etc., are really talking about eternal life. Similarly, the verse "and you shall live by them" can be understood in this way.

We can explain this subject further by examining the philosophical works of the Rishonim

(Medieval Authorities), with a question that was often posed. It is known that the Torah does not explicitly mention any reward except material and physical rewards in this world. Spiritual pursuits, which are the ultimate goal of the Torah, and the satisfaction that one finds in spirituality, are not openly taught in the Torah according to all of the Sages. The Holy Shlah in his pamphlet "Beis Acharon" brings three reasons for this. There is the opinion of the Rambam (Maimonides), z"l; the Ramban (Nachmanides), z"l; and the Ran (Rabbenu Nissim), z"l, in his sermons. There are questions on all of them. See there in the words of the Holy Shlah. In the end, he writes his own opinion, according to an amazing introduction. He says that all of the Names and words in the Torah, and in the Holy Hebrew language in general, have a very high root in a supernal holy place. That is the actual name of a thing. After that, the name descends through a chain down from this holy place. The outcome of this chain is also called by this name, but only in a sense that is "borrowed" from the heavenly source above. See there, where he explains this concept at length. This can explain the philosophical inquiry of the abovementioned Rishonim, as to why spiritual designations are not mentioned in the Torah. The fact is that they are mentioned. It is quite the opposite, as they are mentioned in their essence and not merely in their "borrowed" form. For example, when it says "I will give your rains in their time", etc., these drops of water that fall down are not "geshem"/"rain" in its essential form, but rather there is a spiritual entity that God created above in heaven called "rain". After this, it descends through a spiritual chain through all of the worlds until we have physical "rain", which is only called "rain" in a way "borrowed" from the spiritual entity called "rain". It is really borrowed from one level to the next until this lowest level that we can see. It is the same with any of the promises in the Torah. We see that it is quite the opposite, as it is the spiritual reward that is mentioned explicitly in the Torah. However, as we are still physical and material, we explain these words with material concepts that we can understand. Until here are a few of his words. See there his words at length.

In any event, the Holy Torah includes with all of these physical designations all of these rewards, the reward in this world and the spiritual reward that will come in the world of souls. The simple meaning of Scripture is like a container that clothes the Light of the Torah in physical letters. According to these "garments", we assign these words to name material objects, and the reward in This World. However, the inner point within them speaks of spiritual concepts, as the essence of any word is really speaking of the spiritual aspect of an object's existence. The main thing is the inner meaning of any thing. This is what Rav Kahana said in the Talmud (Shabbos 63a) "when I was eighteen years old, I had already studied the entire Talmud, and I never saw that Scripture could be taken away from its simple meaning." Thus, when it is written "and you shall live by them", even though the main intent is concerning eternal life according to the inner teachings of the Torah, however the simple meaning is also true, and Scripture also intends that "you shall live by them" refers to life in this world as well.

According to this, we can understand this well. Since the Torah was given from Heaven, it is necessary to say that the Torah must have an inner meaning. This is the reason that the angels wanted to receive the Holy Torah. If the Torah is only the physical garments alone, then why would the angels be interested in the Torah, inasmuch as they do not have eating and drinking and the like in their world. Thus, their intent in wanting to have the Torah must have been for the inner aspects of the Torah. Since all Israel together said "we will do and we will listen" at Sinai, it shows that there is also a simple meaning to the Torah as well. This must be so, inasmuch as the simple folk would not have understood the inner aspects of the Torah, however they also agreed to accept the Torah, as it is written "and all of the people answered in unison and said, 'all that the LORD speaks we will do'." It is also written, "Thus shall you say to the house of Jacob and tell to the sons of Israel". It is understood that the "house of Jacob" refers to the simple people, which is why Moses was instructed to tell them these words with a soft form of speech. "The sons of Israel" refers to the more spiritually sophisticated people, and to them Moses was instructed to tell them more harsh words, tough as sinews. This is because the sophisticated people understood the inner aspects of the Torah as well. They saw that it was difficult to understand these matters, thus they had the words that were "tough as sinews". But the simple meaning of the Torah was given to the simple folk, who received it with soft words.

In any event, the Torah was also given to the simple folk, as it is written "and 'all' of the people answered in unison". They all said "we will do and we will listen". Even though the sophisticated people understood the inner aspects of the Torah as well, in any event they also accepted the simple meaning of the Torah. If one were to claim that the sophisticated people only accepted the inner aspects of the Torah, and the simple folk only accepted the simple meanings, then how could it have said "all of the people answered in unison", if they were not all equal in their acceptance of the Torah? Thus, we must say that the simple meaning of the Torah is what unified the entire nation. Even though the sophisticated people understood the deeper meanings of the Torah, in any event, they also accepted the simple meaning of the Torah upon themselves. This is because Scripture never totally leaves its simple meaning. Thus, the Torah must also be learned in a simple way.

Through this, we can come to the subject at hand. It is possible that the Midrash wanted to answer this issue. By the Heavens a harsh terminology was used. By Earth there was soft speech. It says "hear, oh Heavens" because the Torah was given from Heaven, as it is said "you saw that God speaks to you from Heaven". Since the Torah was given from heaven, then there must be an inner meaning to the Torah, which is why the angels desired to receive the Torah, as we said above. From here, we can see that the words "the Heavens" in this verse refer to the spiritually sophisticated people, who grasp the inner aspects of the Torah. Thus, it says by the Heavens "and I will speak", using a harsh terminology, because it is very difficult to grasp the inner aspects of the Torah. "And hear, oh Earth", for the Israelites were standing on the Earth and they said "all that the LORD says we will do and we will listen", and from here it is understood that even the simple folk accepted the simple meanings of the Torah, as we said above. Thus, it is said to the Earth "the speech of my mouth", with soft words, as the simple meaning of the Torah can be considered "soft words".

This is why "and I will speak" is in the future tense, while "the speech of my mouth" is in the present tense. The inner aspects of the Torah are eternal and will remain forever. The more one goes in depth into the Torah, the more one grasps.

This pursuit is endless. Thus, the words "and I will speak" are in the future tense, because this will last forever and this is eternal. However, the simple meanings of the text that refer to material objects will not last forever, because every material object has an end when it will no longer exist. Thus, when it says "the speech of my mouth", it is either in the present tense or the past tense, because it is not eternal.

In any event, we see from here that everything is set in the Torah, both the simple meaning of the Torah and the deeper meaning of the Torah, both material and spiritual designations. Thus, we can learn from "and you shall live by them" that you should not die by them, meaning that a threat to life overrides the Sabbath, even though the inner intention that the Torah has for the Scripture "and you shall live by them" refers to eternal life, because Scripture does not totally deviate from its simple meaning. Thus, the verse also refers to life in this world, as everything is hinted to in the Torah. This is the legal connection from the question as to whether one who has an ear ache may seek healing on the Sabbath to the verse "hear, oh Heaven, and I will speak. And listen, Earth, to the words of my mouth", that the heaven speaks of the inner aspects of the Torah, and the Earth refers to the simple meaning of the Torah, and all in hinted in it. Therefore, we can understand that a threat to life overrides the Sabbath, based on "and you should live by them" and not die by them.

And according to this, all of the prayers we pray for life, "remember us for life", that even if the main point of our prayers is for eternal life, but we need to pray for life in this world as well. Therefore, the intent is also on the simple meaning of life in this world. May God help us that we should be worthy to life in this world and in the next world, and we should be saved from all trouble and sorrow, and we should be worthy to a year of redemption and salvation, and to see the light of the Face of the King of Life in holiness and purity, and we should be worthy to see the salvation and joy of all Israel, and in the elevation of the Glory of Torah and the Jewish people, and in the revelation of the Glory of Heaven upon us, soon and in our days, Amen.

(Divrei Yoel - Parshas Haazinu/Shabbos Shuvah p. 195-197)

PARSHAS VEZOS HABRACHAH

"And Moses was one hundred and twenty years old at his death, and his eyes did not dim"

It is cited in the Sifri, that "we learn from here that the eyes of the dead generally dim". Until here are the words of the Midrash Sifri.

This needs to be explained. When we speak of the dead in general, do not all of their senses cease? Why is the sense of sight different that it should be mentioned here? Also, what is the meaning of "dimming", does not the sense of sight totally end? One may say that this refers to the holy tzaddikim (righteous people), who are called "alive" even after they die. They have a form of sight in their cognitive soul, in order to delight in the Glory of the Shechinah (Divine Presence) in the Supernal Garden of Eden. However, their sense of vision is dimmed, because they cannot see or feel that which is happening in this material world, because their eyes are dimmed so they should not see the suffering of the Jewish people. It is known that my holy ancestor, the Yismach Moshe, zt"l, would often say that the tzaddikim in heaven forget about the troubles of this world due to the greatness of the bright light of Heaven. This is the meaning of the saying that the eyes of the dead are "dimmed", because the tzaddikim continue to see clearly in the Next World, however from the brightness of the glory of Heaven they are blinded from seeing the suffering of the Jewish people on earth, so their eyes are dimmed from seeing. However, "this was not the case with My servant, Moses", because our teacher Moses was the faithful shepherd, the master and savior of Israel. He could never forget his people, even while he is dwelling above on High in the Holiness of the Higher worlds. Moses always sees and feels the suffering of the Jewish people, and prays to God to arouse mercy upon them at all times. This is what Scripture says, "and Moses was one hundred and twenty years old at his death, and his eyes did not dim", the statement concerning the fact that his eyes did not dim is connected to his death, to say that even in his death he will go beneath his honorable stature, and his eyes would not be dimmed at all from seeing the situation of the people of Israel.

(Chiddushei Torah for Simchas Torah 5712/1951 - cited in Machzor Divrei Yoel - Sukkos volume 2 - p. 604)

BEZHY"S

WITH THE HELP OF THE BLESSED LORD

SEFER VAYOEL MOSHE

INTRODUCTION

Inasmuch as, due to our abundant sins, we have endured in the last few years abundant and horribly bitter sufferings, such that the Jewish people have never witnessed before in the entire history of our nation. If it had not been for the

Lord's mercy, there would not have remained a remnant of our people. For with the grace of the Lord, may His Name be blessed, there has remained an extremely small population, not a few from many, but rather a few from a few. This is because of the promise that God swore to our ancestors, that their seed would never be totally destroyed, heaven forbid. Furthermore, due to our abundant sins, we have seen the total fulfillment of the Biblical prophecy, "and the Lord will make your afflictions extraordinary" (Deuteronomy 28:59), to the point where we only now fully understand the meaning of this Scripture. It is indeed an extraordinary wonder, for the wise have lost their wisdom and the discernment of the understanding people has been hidden, and we wait for the time of healing, for behold, it is coming, but we have not yet reached the resting place and the inheritance. Our hearts are broken inside us to many pieces, and we do not have what to console nor encourage us. Rather our eyes are watching toward heaven, with mournful eyes and a sorrowful soul, until the Lord will look down from heaven, and look upon our affliction, and heal our broken and sorrowful hearts in His abundant mercy, may His Name be blessed.

It used to be among the Jewish people in all former generations that if some sorrow befell the Jewish people, they would seek out to understand what sin brought us into this suffering. They would set this to their hearts to mend their ways and repent, and return to the blessed Lord, as we see in Scripture and in the Talmud. In this spirit, after the expulsion from Spain, the holy and pious Rabbi Yoseph Yaavetz the Sefardi, z"l, composed a work entitled "*Or HaChaim*" (ed. note: not to be confused with the famous "*Or HaChaim*" by Rabbi Chaim Ben Attar, which was composed centuries later), based upon this concept, to investigate which sins caused the sufferings of that expulsion. My ancestor, the author of "*Chavos Daas*", zt"l, wrote in his introduction to his commentary on the book of Lamentations that there is not purpose in merely telling over suffering and pain unless one also mentions the reasons for the suffering that befell him, in order to protect oneself from the causes that bring about such suffering. Therefore, he explained the entire book of Lamentations in this manner, that in every place where some pain is mentioned, the sin that brought it about is also mentioned, in order that we should return to the Lord with our entire heart, and no longer cause our own suffering. This is his basic premise in his commentary, which deserves study.

Now, in our generation, we do not need to investigate some hidden sin that brought this suffering upon us, for it is openly brought in the teachings of the Sages, who taught us based on the Bible that by breaking our promises to God not to "ascend as a wall" (meaning conquering the Holy Land), and not to "push the end-times" that "I will", heaven forbid, "permit your flesh as the deer and the antelope of the field are to the hunters". Due to our abundant sins, this has been fulfilled, for the heretics and non-believers have done all kinds of work to violate these oaths, in order to "ascend as a wall" and to make for themselves an independent sovereign state before the proper time, which is the meaning of "pushing the end-times", to try to actualize eschatology through political means. Furthermore, they have dragged the hearts of most of the Jewish people into this impure idea. It is taught in the Mechilta on Parshas Yisro, "why does it say 'Thou shalt not take the Name of the Lord in vain' (Exodus 20:7)? Because elsewhere it says 'you should not swear falsely', from there we would only learn not to swear, but where would we learn not to accept? Once one accepts an oath, I become a Judge to you, for 'He does not absolve anyone who takes His Name in vain'." The *Merkavas HaMishneh* explains there that it seems that when it come to violation of oaths, one is judged on thought, just as is the case with idolatry, not to lessen, but rather to bring closer. The R"I also brings there, that we see the fact that Maimonides does not include this law that this is merely a scriptural hint to a rabbinical decree. This needs much further study, but now is not the time to delve into this discussion.

However, in our case, the violation was not merely mental, to the point that we would be questioning whether one is judged for thought in this matter. Rather, many actions have been done to further this bitter cause, which a miriad of plans and ways to bring about the violation of these oaths. It is clear and simple that each and every one of these actions is considered alone to be a breach of the oath. We can see this from the letter that Maimonides, zt"l, wrote to Yemen, concerning someone in those days in Yemen claiming to be the Messiah. Several people came to Maimonides to ask about this, and he told them that this person is presenting a great danger to the

Jews in Yemen, because when the government will hear about this it will bring about great suffering, may God save us. He also warned them in this letter that they should be careful not to violate these oaths. He writes there that the reason for these oaths is because King Solomon saw with the holy spirit of prophecy that people will try to bring about the end times themselves in the wrong time, and that they will be destroyed because of this, and that suffering will come because of this. See there in Maimonides' letter to Yemen. From this we see that Maimonides knew that the only result of these activities will be suffering. In any event, he considered this to be a violation of the oaths, for when we swore not to push the end-times, it meant that we will do no action whatsoever to push the end-times. Therefore, we see that any action whatsoever that is done for this purpose, even if it is totally doomed to failure, is already considered to be an active violation of the oath. Therefore, it is clear that this is not compared to a mere thought, for according to the *Merkavas HaMishnah* there this is only a scriptural hint to a rabbinical opinion as far as thought is concerned. However actual deeds are certainly considered to be an active violation of the oaths, and not mere thoughts.

It is taught in the Talmud, Tractate Shevuos, page 39, that when any of the sins of the Torah are violated, only the sinner himself has to pay for it, but when an oath is violated the sinner's family and the entire world has to pay for it. We see from this that violating an oath is such a grave sin that the entire world is punished when only one individual is guilty of violating an oath. All the more so when there are so many actions to this goal done by many people, to the point where in the last few years one could almost say that the majority of the Jewish people are aiding this cause in different ways that result in violation of the oaths. Furthermore, these sins are done publicly in the sight of the entire Jewish people, and the number of people who have properly rebuked this sin are extremely small. That is why this suffering has befallen us, in accord with what the Sages taught that they are made ownerless like deer and antelope of the field, may the Merciful One save us. And, "disaster only befalls the world because of the wicked and it only begins from the righteous". And if this were the only sin the Jewish people were guilty of, it is already open plainly in the teachings of the Sages that this would be the bitter punishment. The children of

Ephraim were holy saints, however, because of the sin of leaving the exile before the time, that what happened to them in the middle of their trip. The sages teach that this was because they violated the oaths, even though it was accidental, because they made a mistake in calculating the proper time. Also, in the time of Ben Koziba, it was a generation filled with Torah and holiness in an amazing way, and yet they were punished with abundant deaths, may the Merciful One save us, to a toll even higher than was in the time of the destruction of the Temple, as is explained many times in the words of the Sages, for example in the Jerusalem Talmud it says that at that time the pride of Israel was cut off and will not be returned until the Son of David comes. In the Midrash Rabbah on Song of Songs it says concerning the Scripture, "I make you swear...", that because of the violation of this oath came the downfall in the time of Ben Koziba. I will expound upon this further inside the book, but from contemplating this point alone one can understand the severity of the consequences of violating this oath.

In the Talmud, Tractate Yevamos p. 78b, it says concerning the verse "and there was a famine in the days of David for three years" (II Samuel 21:1) that after the first year it was asked, "perhaps there is the sin of idolatry in our midst? As it says 'and you will serve other gods... and you will not have rain' (Deuteronomy 11)." They investigated the matter, and did not find any idolatry. The second year it was asked "maybe there are wanton sinners in our midst, as is written (in Jeremiah 3)", they investigated, and did not find any wanton sinners. The third year it was asked, "perhaps those who publicly ask for charity are not being given enough, as is written (in Proverbs 25)", this too was investigated, and was not found either. The Urim and Tumim were finally consulted. The answer was given "it is because of Saul and his bloody house" (II Samuel 21:1). The Ri"f asks many questions on this. His main question why did they not immediately consult the Urim and Tummim, and put a stop to the famine immediately, as they did after the three years? Why did they need to wait three years to investigate these three sins, causing the Jewish people to suffer three years of famine due to the lack of knowledge of what they needed to rectify, rather than immediately asking the Urim and Tumim? The Maharsh"a writes that they thought that there was some sin in their midst, whether it be idolatry, immorality, or lack of charity, which are things which do not involve the government. The rule is that only the king may inquire of the Urim and Tumim, that is when it is something relative to his government. We do not understand this answer yet, because they did not know whether someone in their midst violated one of these three sins, and this is bolstered by the fact that after three years of investigation they did not find any instance of these sins. The entire time it was only a lack of knowledge, only a doubt as to what was the cause of the famine, as is obvious from the wording of the Talmud "maybe there is among us". Therefore, in the case of doubt, there was reason to suspect that the reason could have been a governmental issue, as in the end it turned out in fact to be so. It would seem that in the case of any doubt, the Urim and Tumim should be consulted first, in order to spare the Jewish people from suffering three years of famine, so why did they wait to do so until they spent three years investigating the possible sins, that they did not find in the end? The Ri"f explains this there at length, and the summation of his words are that until a thorough investigation was made, it was to be assumed that one of these three sins were the cause of the famine, because Scripture attests that these sins bring about famine, see there for the length of his words. However, this still needs some more study, because we still do not understand fully. In any event, we see that even in the time when our people did have access to the Urim and Tumim, they always assumed that the answer to their question could be that mentioned in Scripture, rather than consulting the Urim and Tumim. However, elsewhere throughout Scripture we never see such a horrible and bitter punishment as "I will permit your flesh", as in literally ownerless and free, "like the deer and the antelope of the field", except for this one sin of pushing the end-times and violating the oath, like the Scripture says, "I make you swear", to which the Sages teach the above teaching of "I will permit". Such suffering has never touched the Jewish people in the entire history of our nation, except for in our generation, due to our abundant sins. Every other time in history there was some decree to abandon our faith, or something similar, however in this generation there was no reason given, but was simply a release of our blood to be free for the kill, like deer and antelope of the field, and we had no idea why this was happening. Therefore, we see that it must be attributed to that which is openly mentioned in Scripture, which states that such a punishment only comes from violating those oaths, therefore the Scripture comes to attest that this is the reason. However, no one pays attention nor sets this to heart.

See the commentary of the Ramba"n (Nachmanides) on the Book of Exodus, Parshas Ki Tisa, in several of the verses, where he explains that those who actually worshipped the golden calf were very few in number, but most of the nation sinned in some way in their mind. Therefore, there was a force of anger from God to destroy the entire nation, heaven forbid. The meaning of the verse "and the Lord was angry... because they made the calf", from which we see that the anger was not only against those who bowed down to the calf or brought sacrifices to it, but even to those who made it, meaning those who gathered around Aaron and those who brought him gold, and he brings concerning this the words of the Targum, [where the Aramaic translation of the words "because they made the calf" could also be interpreted as] "because they served the calf". This means that the Divine Wrath was not only because of those, very few people, who actually worshipped the calf, through actions of offering sacrifices and bowing to it, but mostly due to the majority of the people, who assisted in making it, by gathering with them or by donating gold, and the like. This was because they thought that this was a good thing, [not for the sake of idolatry, but rather] for the sake of having a leader to guide their way, in the place of Moses [who they thought had died], all in the Name of Hashem (God), as has been explained in depth by the Ramban, the Ibn Ezra, the Baalei Tosafos, and other *Rishonim* (Medieval

Rabbinical Authorities), of blessed memory. Similarly, this bitter "calf" of making a government before the coming of the Messiah, for this impure philosophy began many years before making the State, through the Zionists, who did many actions in many ways for the sake of violating these oaths. Due to our abundant sins, most of our nation, in the various groups among the Zionists, were middle men and interceders to help this goal. Even among the kosher Jews, who fought a great deal against the Zionists, because of their deeds, including their uprooting of religion, their heresy and apostacy, may the Merciful God save us, however in the actual impure idea of their, of going free and making a government before the coming of the Messiah, which is the main root of bitterness and poisonous sadness, in this idea many of the Kosher Jews were trapped, because the power of the Evil Urge is great, for it blinds the eyes in this regard. And they did not set this to heart, and instead they helped this evil thing, from most of the people, some by deeds, some by speech in various ways, for their eyes were closed from seeing, for their soul was in it. It is not my will to elaborate on this point, to explain it fully, however if one meditates upon this he can know the truth. In the incident of the trespass of Achan [recorded in the book of Joshua], there was Divine Wrath upon the entire people of Israel, because of one sinner who was not properly rebuked, how much more so in this present-day plague, which has infected most of the Jewish people, due to our abundant sins. And God does not judge without justice, and we see that Scripture openly shows what is the punishment of this awesome sin of violating these oaths, and we see it has been fulfilled. And according to what I will, God willing, write inside of this work, will explain at length how this entire concept of taking a government for Israel before the coming of the Messiah is one that is essentially filled with heresy and apostacy away from the ways of the Blessed Lord, because only He is the Master (Who enslaves us into Exile) and Redeemer (Who brings us back home), and there is none but Him, may His Name be blessed, our Redeemer, even in the days of the Messiah. Such a concept, which is wrought with heresy and apostacy, may the Merciful One save us, certainly damages even to the point of the intellect, because heresy is worse than idolatry, as is taught in the Talmud and by Maimonides, as is known, and all the more so [if it goes beyond the levels of thought and] if many actions are done among the Children of Israel, due to our abundant sins.

However, despite all of this, and even more, for these sects have brought about this impure idea of establishing a government before the proper time without the mandate of the Torah, and they have drawn most of the Children of Israel into awful heresy and apostacy, that there never was since the world came to be, inasmuch as even the (non-Jewish) peoples of the world, who serve idols, believe in HASHEM, Who is the blessed Lord, and that He is the Original Cause of all. However, these evil people deny even the very foundation of faith. First they draw people in with that "which is desirable to the eyes" (Genesis 3:6), to be "like all the nations" (I Samuel 8:20) to have a people and a government like the (non-Jewish) peoples. Then they went even further to draw them into their apostacy that there is no judgement and no Judge, God forbid, that all is dependent upon mortal strength and weapons of war. There is no need to expound upon this at length, because it is obvious what type of awful revolution these sects have caused, may the Merciful One save us, for they have turned many countries to apostacy, and have spread the power of heresy in full force to many Jewish homes, including religious homes, to an immeasurable level. Literally a large sum of millions of Jews have fallen by their hands into the net of heresy, may the Merciful One save us. And through the fact that many sects have joined them who say their intent in joining together with them is to repair them, by bringing into these heretics also the way of the Torah, this was the trap that caught many Kosher Jews into the clutches of this unclean ideology, that made them think that by (seeing that Orthodox leaders tried the fix the State they actually opposed, many Jews though that actually they were doing a mitzvah by) supporting the establishment of the State they thought that they were actually doing something to support the cause of Torah, and afterwards they fell completely into the trap of heresy via the bridge that the religious Jews made in connecting themselves with the Zionists. This sort of heresy definitely damages the mind. Anyone who thinks they can follow after these sects will fall mentally into an ideology which is essentially rooted in heresy, may the Merciful One save us. Even if he does not feel this initially in his mind, but the "end of a deed begins with a thought".

The general concept is: besides the serious transgression of violating the oath, they also defiled the House of Israel with heresy and apostacy, may the Merciful One save us, therefore it is not surprising that there was such an outpouring of anger and indignation from the LORD, as the Scripture warns us in Parshas Nitzavim (Deuteronomy 29:17-20). Also, during this destruction, the most pious servants of the Most High were murdered, due to the sins of the sinners and the causers of sin, due to our abundant iniquities, and the Divine Wrath was very abundant. (Besides the fact that the Zionists themselves performed various deeds to bring about all of this evil, thinking that through this it would further their design to establish a government and state, and they hoped to build our people on top of this destruction. I wrote a little about this inside of the pamphlet, but I did not see it fit to expand upon this subject in this pamphlet, which is specifically aimed to clarify everything with clear proofs and evidence, and I only came to compose this pamphlet in order to clarify the opinion of Torah). And the remnant of the Children of Israel that God allowed to remain, because of His promise to never allow his (Jacob's) progeny to go extinct, were also punished with a harsh and bitter punishment, inasmuch as this Satanic act was successful in establishing a heretical regime in order to tempt Israel with such a tremendous test as this. Like is explained by the Rava"h, in Parshas Re'eh, on the verse "and the sign or the wonder come to pass" (Deuteronomy 13:3), "for He is testing you" (Deuteronomy 13:4), as the reason that the Lord your God is testing you is in order to remain with Him and that He should not kill you. It is explained from this that the difficult test comes from the success of such a prophecy, that "the sign or the wonder come to pass", and that this is a punishment to Israel that they allowed (this false prophet) to say such words of prophecy. Now, it is all the more so (a problem) when most of Israel is aiding these sects, because this (the support of the Jewish people) gives the *Samech-Mem* (the Satan) the power to show such a sign and a wonder. This is also what the Holy *Or HaChaim* writes on his commentary to Parshas Yisro, on the verse "You should have no other gods" (Exodus 20:3), that by worshiping a false god one causes that "god" to have some existence as a "god" what it did not have before it was believed in or worshipped. So God allowed the Zionists to test the Jewish people, but due to our abundant sins the majority were not able to stand up against this difficult test, similar to the way that in the days of the First

Temple there was a difficult temptation toward idolatry, and in the days of Gideon there were only three hundred men in all of Israel who did not bow to Baal, and through these few men there was a great revival of penitence in Israel, as is explained in Scripture. And presently, in this low generation at the footsteps of the Messianic era, people still have not set to heart that all of the suffering and sorrows that have fallen upon us were because of these wicked people. And we need to return to the Blessed Lord and run away from them and their multitudes more than one runs away from a lion that is pursuing after one to kill him, and anything that is possible to save even one Jewish soul from alliance with them, it is immensely valuable to a level that is immeasurable, in taking the valuable gem out of the garbage. They are turning over against the word of the Living God and are blaming the troubles on those who listen to the voice of the Holy Torah, as has been the path of the heretics from ancient times. It is clearly explained in Jeremiah 44:18 when the cursed women said "since we stopped sacrificing to the queen of heaven... we have lacked all things, and have been consumed by the sword and by famine", then blaming all of their troubles on the prophets of the LORD who warned them not to worship idolatry, and Jeremiah cried out to them that their sin has caused all of their troubles, and subsequently clarified the words of the prophets to be true and just. Now, anyone who has a brain in his skull can recognize the truth that it is only the sin of those who cause others to stumble in this sinful and unclean idea (of Zionism) have brought all of the troubles and tribulations, due to our abundant sins, upon the Children of Israel, as I will write concerning this within the book. --- And it is brought in Noam Elimelech in the "Sacred Epistle" that when our patriarch Abraham, peace be upon him, came to the Land of Israel and there came about a famine in the land, the inhabitants of that location said, that because of this heretic we had this misfortune fall upon us, and he went down to Egypt to escape legal recourse that they (the Canaanites) sought among themselves against him. It was specifically concerning our current generation that our Sages remarked "those who fear sin will be despised" (Sotah 49b), and many more similar statements that I have brought within the book, and there is no point in elaborating on the tremendous amount of lies and falsehood from these brazen and arrogant people, may the Merciful One save us, and he who believes in the

Blessed LORD and in His Torah knows the truth.

And this is clear, that this abominable idea (Zionism) is the deterrence of our redemption and the salvation of our souls, as I have brought inside of the book the words of the Midrash Yalkut on Parshath Bo: Remez 191, on the verse "And it shall be for you to guard" (Exodus 12:6) the Midrash says "Who rescued you from Medea?... Mordecai and Esther. Who rescued you from the Greeks?... the Hasmoneans. Who will save you from the fourth kingdom? *Natruna* (Patience). This is the meaning of 'and it shall be for you to guard, do not eat from it raw', meaning it one should not impatiently ask that it should be left uncooked." The *Zaith Raanan* and the *Magen Avraham* explain that the Aramaic word "*natruna*" means that we have to keep it and wait patiently, "do not ask it to be left uncooked" means that one should not ask to eat of it when it is still raw, meaning it has not been sufficiently roasted. It is thus explained by this that we do not presently have any other merit to leave the exile, other than the merit of waiting patiently, not to eat of it raw, God forbid, and not to benefit from a "redemption" such as this which comes before the appointed time. And therefore, all of those who take hold of their rope, with a portion in them and their government, and eating together with these abominable people, are doing so against the Scriptural warning of "do not eat from it raw", it is they who are holding back the redemption. I also brought the words of the Talmud in Sanhedrin p. 98a, that "the Son of David will not come until the lowest government ceases from Israel," which Rashi of blessed memory explains, "that the Israelites should have no sovereignty, even the sovereignty of a weak and insignificant government." It is clearly stated that before the Messiah comes that that insignificant government will cease to exist, for it is impossible for him to come in any other manner, and it (the government's existence) is that which is preventing the redemption. Similarly, we find the same idea clearly comes out of the words of Maimonides' "Epistle to Yemen". Rather we need Heavenly Mercy that that government will be eliminated only through a Supernal Force from the Blessed LORD, and not through the work of the nations, because if it will be, God forbid, through the military work of the nations there will be a tremendous danger to Israel, as is understood, and the Blessed LORD will have mercy upon us and upon His entire people Israel. In any event, anyone who benefits from or receives accolades from that government, they are receiving benefit from prevention of the Messiah's coming, and woe to them for such an embarrassment and such shame.

Since the redemption is dependent upon this concept, the *Yetzer Hara* (Evil Inclination) and the *Samech-Mem* (Satan) have strengthened their efforts to such a degree that they have pulled the entire world into this spiritually-disqualified philosophy. This is like the *Tosafoth Yom Tov* writes in Tractate Avoth chapter 5 concerning the Mishnah that calculates the miracles that took place in the Temple, and includes among them the miracle that the High Priest never experienced a seminal emission on Yom Kippur (the Day of Atonement), and he writes concerning this: "there are those who question why would the High Priest experience an emission after they encouraged him to remain pure all seven days leading up to the Day, and he was in a state of purity on that entire Day, and the old people would talk to him all night to keep him awake? The answer is that the *Yetzer HaTov* (the Good Inclination) and the *Yetzer HaRa* (the Evil Inclination) are fighting with each other like two foes, and when one of them is close to victory, the other strengthens itself against its attacker, seeing that he is about to be consumed by evil, etc. That is why the High Priest was actually close to having an emission that would disqualify the service, and thus a miracle was needed to avoid it." See there for more. If this was so then, it is all the more so now, as we stand right before the redemption, and it is known that after the redemption the *Yetzer HaRa* and the *Samech-Mem* will be nullified, and there will be a total victory against them in a way that has never been since the day the world was created, as is also taught by *Tosafoth* in Tractate Rosh Hashanah p. 16b beginning with the word "*K'dai*" that the Jerusalem Talmud teaches that after the Great Shofar is sounded it will come the time for the Satan to be devoured, therefore it is certain that he will strengthen himself with all levels of courage and might against any concept that brings about the redemption, and one needs miracles of miracles to be saved from it, much more than the miracle that was required for the High Priest to be spared from an emission on Yom Kippur. That is why the *Samech-Mem* (Satan) set up the Zionist State and the heretical government to nullify the redemption, and the Blessed LORD will have mercy upon us soon and cause for us the time of our redemption and the salvation of our souls.

In the Midrash Eichah Rabbah 3:19 on the verse "This I recall to my heart, therefore have I hope." (Lamentations 3:21) it is written at the end and this is the text: "the day after the end of the redemption comes, the Holy One Blessed is He will say to Israel, 'My son, I am amazed by you that you have waited so long for me all of those years', and they will say before Him, 'Master of the World, if it were not for the Torah You gave us we would have already been assimilated into the nations.' that is why it says "'this' I recall to my heart", for "this" refers only to the Torah, as it is written "and this is the Torah" (Deuteronomy 4:44), and thus did David say "if not for Your Torah, which was my delight, then I would have been destroyed in my poverty" (Psalm 119:92). "Therefore, I have hope..." see there in the Midrash where it elaborates in the beginning with a parable. We see from this that to wait and hope for the redemption is a tremendous test, so much so that God Himself will say to the Israelites afterward that He is amazed that they withstood the challenge of the test, and it is impossible to withstand this test without setting one's heart upon the Holy Torah, and only the Holy Torah will protect us and save us.

The truth is that all heretical paths, may God save us, prevent the redemption, as is explained in the Talmud in Rosh Hashanah p. 17a, "The sectarians and heretics who deny the Torah and the resurrection of the dead, etc. will go down to *Gehinom* (Hell or Purgatory) and be judged there for generations upon generations. Hell will cease to exist yet they will not cease to exist (and continue being judged), as it says 'and their identity will be swallowed up in the netherworld.' (Psalm 49:15) And why such an extreme punishment? Because they set their hands to attack the heavenly abode known as '*Zvul*', as it says, 'so there should be no habitation (*Zvul*) for it' (ibid.). And '*Zvul*' refers only to the Holy Temple, as it says 'and I surely built You a Temple Abode (*Zvul*).' (I Kings 8:13)" Rashi explains "they set their hands to attack *Zvul*" as meaning they destroyed the Holy Temple with their sin. Maimonides brings these words in Chapter 3 of the "Laws of Repentance", but he adds the following of his own words, "and those who deny the coming of the Redeemer". It would seem that it is not clearly understood why the Talmud says the Holy Temple was destroyed by their sin? First of all, we do not find that heresy was one of the sins that the Talmud lists as being responsible for the destruction of the Holy Temple, for the First Temple was destroyed by the sin of idolatry, and the Second Temple was destroyed by the sin of baseless hatred, we do not find any mention anywhere that the Temple was destroyed because of sectarianism or heresy. Furthermore, even if we say there was also a sin of heresy, we would have to say that this only applied to the heretics and sectarians who existed in the Temple era, but since this statement was made during the era of the Talmudic Sages in their time and era, and Maimonides, of blessed memory, also brings it, therefore the statement is relevant to all heretics and sectarians which are in all of the generations. And furthermore it is impossible to say that this only applied to the heretics of the Temple era, because if this were so, what difference would it make to us, as what was done was done, and the Third Temple will never be destroyed again, as is known and mentioned in the Talmud Tractate Megillah concerning the order of our liturgy in the *Shemonah Esrei* prayer, that the heretics and sectarians will cease to exist before the Temple is built, and if that is so, how can it be said that this is plainly referring to all of the heretics and sectarians in all generations and all periods if the reason that the punishment is so harsh upon them is because they stretched out their hands to the heavenly abode (*Zvul*), which is the Holy Temple? Is it not so that we have not had the Holy Temple for close to two millennia? How is it possible to say that they have stretched their hands to attack something that does not exist at all?

We must then answer this according to the statement of our Sages that "any generation in which the Holy Temple was not rebuilt in its days is as if it were destroyed in its days" (Jerusalem Talmud: Tractate Yoma 1:1), and the sectarians and heretics prevent the Holy Temple from being built with their sins, therefore it is as if they have destroyed it, and because of this they are considered in the Talmud as having stretched their hands to attack the Heavenly Abode. If this is so, it is possible to say that, according to the teaching that the Heavenly Temple is built through the divine service of the righteous people and their good deeds, and when the Heavenly Temple is built then our true Messiah will come, however the wicked through their deeds cause destruction in the Heavenly Temple above, and demolish that which the righteous have built there with their good deeds. One time, our holy master, the Rebbe from Sanz, author of Divrei Chaim, (Rabbi Chaim Halberstam) of righteous memory, said at his Pure Table (Tish), that the Holy Temple Above was practically complete, only the Curtain (Parokhes) was missing. The Holy Rebbe, Rabbi Joshua of Tomoshov, of righteous memory, answered, "We believe with absolute faith that you, our holy Rebbe (Rabbi Chaim Halberstam of Sanz), are able to fashion the Temple's Curtain. The author of Divrei Chaim, of righteous memory, did not answer anything at that time. Rather, on another occasion, when he was sitting at his Table (Tish), he began to say, "How do you all know that I did not make the *Parokhes*-Curtain, but a greatly wicked individual tore it with his deeds?" It is explained in the Talmud Tractate Hagigah p. 12, concerning the seven heavenly firmaments, that on the firmament level called "*Zvul*", there is the Heavenly Jerusalem, the Holy Temple, and the Altar built, and if that is so, however the wicked with their sins cause damage right up to the heart of heaven in the firmament called "*Zvul*" where the Heavenly Jerusalem and the Holy Temple exist, and are causing destructions there, may the Merciful One save us, through their sins, and they are stretching their hands to attack the Divine Abode known as "*Zvul*", and they are causing destruction there. Therefore, the *Samech-Mem* (Satan) has overpowered the world to drag them after those who are destroying the Abode known as "*Zvul*", and is causing the people to err and to say that they are the saviors, in order to prevent the Redemption through this. Heaven trembles over this, and it will be explained more inside this book at length.

In the book *Zera Kodesh* from Ropshitz, it is written in Parshas Ki Teitzei on the verse "when you build a new house" (Deuteronomy 22:8), "According to that which is explained concerning the words of our liturgy 'and rebuild it soon by our days as an eternal building,' that 'the Lord will build Jerusalem' (Psalm 147:2), and what will He build it with? 'By our days', meaning through our 'days', that every day that a person serves God, all according to one's deeds, one builds Jerusalem and the Holy Temple, thus a Jewish person who serves the Lord every day until the Temple will be built completely, soon and in our days." Similar have I heard in the name of the Holy Rebbe, our Master Rabbi Elimelech from Lizhensk, of righteous and sacred memory, that when he would use meditative techniques to cause his soul to ascend to the higher realms, he would see that they were carrying the vessels from the Holy Temple, and they told him that they were the same vessels that he took from the Exile. One time he said that a large House of Impurity (Idolatrous Temple or Church) fell down with a very large idol, and every day millions of workers were coming to build the wall, "but I have a good guardian, that is when the Rebbe, our master Rabbi Jacob Isaac from Lantzhut (The Seer from Lublin) prays the daily *Shemonah Esrei* prayer during the Afternoon Service, he knocks down all that they are building," and I understood from his holy words that this was knocked down by him, because through his prayers he is building the walls of Jerusalem and the Holy Temple, and according to the measure of his building the walls of Jerusalem, that is the measure that he is destroying this house of impurity, for when this (the Holy Temple) is raised that (the idolatrous temple) falls." Until here are his holy words. Through this we can understand how the wicked are bringing destruction to the Heavenly Holy Temple above, because it is in direct opposition to their forces of impurity, and may the Lord have mercy.

And behold, I have seen that the root of this error that has been dragged into this world, that the first cause is because there has not been sufficient study into the depth of the words explaining this law of the Three Oaths (Talmud Kethuboth 111a), that people do not realize how far these words reach concerning the awesome prohibition against taking a government before the proper time has arrived. Therefore, their desires did not overpower them to be like all of the nations, a people and a government against our religion. – Furthermore, they have also found sources for a weak basis to join together with them (the Zionists), even though they are heretics and deniers, inciters and enticers seeking to draw us away from the true path, however they think it was also like this in the period of Ahab and Manasseh, and Heaven forbid they have permitted the strap holding them back to allow them to join with such a government. And all of this comes from the temptations of the evil inclination, and heresy is different as it draws one on (Talmud Avodah Zarah 27b), as will be explained within. And behold, the main foundation of the prohibition against violating the Three Oaths is not so clearly explained in the Codes of Law like other laws that are to be found every day and in every generation. This is like what the Tur wrote in *Yoreh Deah* chapter 332, concerning the laws of agrarian tributes such as gleanings, forgotten stalks, and the corners of fields, that since today we are not accustomed to their practice, since most of our neighbors are gentiles, therefore he was not willing to speak about these laws at length, even though it is certainly possible that in some generation there would be some locations where Jews would own fields and most of their neighbors would not be gentiles, like it is today in the Land of Israel in many locations, however since this was not the case in his period he was not willing to treat these laws at length. And for a further explanation, the Tur writes in the beginning of chapter 331, concerning the laws of *Terumah* offerings and agricultural Tithes, that since those laws do not apply outside of the Holy Land, he did not want to treat them at length, even though they certainly applied in that time in the Land of Israel, for the Codifiers did not find it pressing to explain anything other than what was practiced in their time and in their location.

And it seems that this is according to what is written in the introduction to "*Chovos HaLevavos*" (Duties of the Heart), that one of the sages asked a strange question concerning divorce, and he goes on to admonish and embarrass this sage for this, for is it not sufficient for him that he has not yet perfected his soul with all of the pieces of knowledge that are necessary that a person has an obligation to never hide from them at any time, why should he burden himself with a strange question? The *Chovos HaLevavos* discusses this at length, as well as the commentators on it, see there. And it seems that this is the reason why it was their way to only explain the laws that were practiced in their time and place, for the Holy Torah is longer than the Earth's measure and the hearts are limited in their understanding, that it is impossible to stand upon perfect knowledge even on those issues that are needed to know at each and every moment, therefore they did not want to further burden their readers with issues that were not observed in their time, in order to avoid cutting off those issues that were needed to know at that time. And our Sages taught in Bava Metzia p. 114b, that "we did not find among four, but among six we did find!" And

Rashi, of righteous memory, explains that "this is an exclamation of wonder, for the laws of *Zeraim* (Agriculture) are not practiced outside of the Holy Land, nor the laws of *Taharoth* (Levitical Purity)". And in the Responsa *Lechem Rav* we find that in locations where the government did not allow the Jews to adjure cases of monetary laws according to Torah law, even the greatest Rabbis of those locations were not proficient in monetary laws, since they did not deal with them.

And this concept of awakening a movement to violate these Oaths we did not find any case of it from the era of Ben Koziba until the era of Maimonides, which was close to one thousand years, and similarly from the era of Maimonides until the days of Shabbetai Tzvi, and also after the time of Shabbetai Tzvi we did not find it until now in our present generation. In any event, many centuries have passed and changed when it was never found that any person should think to violate this at all, and no one even thought about it at all. Therefore, it automatically became an issue that would not be found to study, and therefore none of the codifiers of all of these generations saw any need to explain this concept in their times, and therefore it is not clearly explained in the Codes. However, anyone who sets their heart upon the words of those Medieval Codifiers (*Poskim Rishonim*) and they great later authorities (*Gedolei HaAcharonim*) who speak about this, they will find that their words are clear to eliminate the possibility to err in this matter. And this is certainly because these Oaths are set laws without any disagreement, for Rabbi Judah in the end of Talmud Tractate Kethuboth was the one who novelized the concept that even an individual may not go up to the Land, as he learned from these Oaths, and Rabbi Zeira, who disagreed with Rabbi Judah on this law, toiled there in the Talmud to satisfy and explain the Oaths according to his view, however it is impossible to say that anyone disagrees that the Oaths exist, rather everyone agrees and admits to them as legally binding as these are major laws, with severe and bitter consequences, may the Merciful One save us, as we do not find such a severe punishment as this on any sin recorded in the entire Torah! Therefore, I set it to my heart to record on paper the explanation of this subject with all of its details and all of the ramifications relating to this sovereign state, and joining with it, and also taking part in their elections, and what comes out of all of this in clear legal definitions according to the Truth of Torah.

And behold, there is much more that what is written here concerning this concept, as it is impossible to record it all on paper, especially in my own personal situation in this present time, as it requires an abundant amount of extra effort far beyond my own capabilities, however as the Lord's Grace is upon me, my hands have been able to produce this minor contribution which I have worked and toiled upon, as I have no time nor a heart with capabilities to bring these items into their proper order, and it is possible that occasionally I have written at length in a manner that is not so orderly, and occasionally I have been more terse, but with all of this I hope that people will find that after contemplating deeply all of the things I have written, that they will have some purpose taken from my words. And if it is accomplished that through my hands I can be worthy to rescue even one Jew from the dungeon of this evil philosophy (of Zionism), then it was all worthwhile, for if we take all of the immorality of this generation and the abundant sins that are committed in the entire world and place them on one end of a scale, and place the Zionist State on the other side, it (Zionism) will out way them all, for it is "a root that bears gall and wormwood" (Deuteronomy 29:17) of the grandfather of impurity of all the major sources of damage in the entire world, and they are the very ones who defile the entire world.

And with this miniscule amount that I have written, I have brought abundant reasons to demonstrate the intensity of the awesome prohibition against joining together with them and of going to their elections, and within this there are many more countless issues that are impossible to be recorded on paper by their sheer volume, however even one who contemplates the words I have already written, even if there remains only one of the reasons I have written, it is sufficient to understand the gravity of the prohibition there is in this thing. However, in my opinion, all of the words I have written are very clear, because I have not written any of my own personal opinions, but I have rather collected all of this from the words of Our Sages, of blessed memory, and from the words of the Gedolim of the Rishonim and Acharonim (great Torah authorities of medieval and modern times), with a limited amount of explanation and understanding of their words, with an occasional smattering of

Pilpul in small amounts, as is the path of Torah as far as what useful information concerning our subject can be taken from this Pilpul, however I did not write long *Pilpulim*, but rather brief explanations pertaining to the clear explanation of the subjects discussed.

And I already said concerning that which Our Sages said in the Talmud, Tractate Shabbath page 55, that "A good measure never goes from God's Mouth and returns to evil except this one..." (see: Ezekiel 9:4) "The attribute of Judgement said before God, 'how are these different than those?', to which He said to her, 'these are totally righteous and those are totally wicked,' she said to Him, 'Lord of the Universe! They (the righteous) should have protested against them (the wicked), yet they did not protest!' He said to her, 'I know, however, as it is revealed before me that if they would have protested against them they would not have accepted the rebuke,' she answered before Him, 'if it is revealed before You, who revealed it before them?' etc. 'and from my Sanctuary' (Ezekiel 9:6)... etc. Rabbi Joseph taught, do not read 'from my Sanctuary' but rather 'from my Holy Ones', these are the people who fulfill the entire Torah from Aleph to Tav." --- And this seems difficult to understand, because if it says they fulfilled the entire Torah from Aleph to Tav, if they failed to protest against sin then they did not fulfill the positive commandment of "you shall surely rebuke your neighbor" (Leviticus 19:17), thus they would be missing this precept from their fulfillment of the entire Torah. Nachmanides in Parshas Savo on the verse "Cursed be he that does not fulfill all of the words of this law" (Deuteronomy 27:26), and he brings from the Jerusalem Talmud that this indicates that one is required to support the Torah out of the hands of those who nullify it, that such a one is cursed, see there. Therefore, we see that this commandment is more serious than the other commandments, and similarly in Sotah page 37b we see that two thousand covenants were carved with the blessings and {p. 12} curses of the cooperative agreement unifying the nation, and this agreement obligates us to protest a breach of the agreement. In any event, this commandment is certainly not less than the other commandments, therefore how can one say concerning them (the righteous people Ezekiel mentions) that they fulfilled the entire Torah from Aleph until Tav?

And I said to answer that it says in the Talmud

Arkhin page 16b that there is a disagreement as to how far the commandment of rebuke extends. Rav says that it goes until the point where the sinner will strike the one offering rebuke, whereas Shmuel says it only goes until the point of cursing, whereas Rabbi Yochanan says it is only to the point of a minor ban (nezifah - a very minor form of excommunication one can place upon another). Similarly, the Talmud records a Tannaic dispute (a dispute among the earlier Rabbis, those of the Mishah era) between Rabbi Eliezer, Rabbi Joshua, and Ben Azai with the same opinions cited. Maimonides in the Laws of *Deioth* (Temperaments) Chapter 6, law 7, he rules like Rav that one must rebuke until the point where the offender will strike the one giving rebuke. The *SMA"G* (*Sefer Mitzvos Gadol* - Great Book of Commandments) questions Maimonides' ruling, because the rule is that whenever Rav and Rabbi Yochanan disagree, the practice follows Rabbi Yochanan, therefore he rules like Rabbi Yochanah that it is only until *Nezifah*. There in the *Hagaos Maimoni* it is written that there is a proof to Maimonides' opinion in Medrash Tanhuma Parshas Tazria that says: "the Attribute of Judgement said 'what is the difference between these from those?' etc. Until, despite that this is so, they should have allowed themselves to be insulted and accepted upon themselves beatings from the Israelites, just as the prophets suffered, for Jeremiah and Isaiah suffered many pains from the Israelites, as it is written, 'I gave my back to those who smite, [and my checks to them that plucked off the hair; I hid not my face from shame and spitting.]' (Isaiah 50:6). Immediately, God went back and said to the destroying angels

['Destroy old and young...' (Ezekiel 9:6)]..." (Until here are the words of the Midrash). It is understood from this that their righteousness was lacking inasmuch as they did not suffer pain of smiting like those prophets, and we see from this that they did indeed protest against the wicked, only they did not protest to the point where they would be physically attacked, because if they did not protest at all it would have said "more than this, they did not protest at all", but from what was said it is apparent that their failure was inasmuch as they did not suffer physical attack, and this is the crux of the dispute, for according to the opinion of Ben Azzai and Rabbi Yochanan, according to whom the SMA"G rules, then they did fulfill the precept of rebuke, even though they did not do so to the point of physical retribution. And it is known that when the Attribute of Mercy and of Kindness are ruling in the world, we depend upon the lenient opinions, therefore prior to the advent of the rule of the Attribute of Strict Justice in the world, it was said concerning these that they fulfilled the entire Torah from Aleph until Tav, according to the (lenient) opinions of Ben Azzai and Rabbi Yochanah, for the truth is "both this and that are the words of the Living God" (Babylonian Talmud Eruvin 13b, et al.), as it is so with all of the disputes of the Tannaim and Amoraim, but when the Attribute of Strict Justice became the ruling force in the world the strict opinion became the law of the time, thus necessitating the precept of rebuke to be until the point of violent physical reaction, for Maimonides also ruled thus, and according to this they did not fulfill their obligation of protest, for it was not to the point of physical retribution by the sinners against the protestors, therefore the Attribute of Strict Justice overtook them on account of the fact that they "did not protest". And we see from here how far these concepts reach.

And Rabbi Moses Maimonides, of blessed memory, writes in the book "Guide to the Perplexed", Section 3, Chapter 29, concerning the interactions between our Patriarch Abraham, peace be upon him, with the people of his generation, and this is a quote from the middle of his words on the subject: "There is no doubt by me concerning him (Abraham), peace be upon him, that when he disagreed with the opinions of all the other people, that those fools cursed him, embarrassed him, and insulted him. However, he accepted all of this for the sake of the Name of the Lord, and it is the law that one must do so for His

Glory" (until here are his holy words). There is seemingly what to understand from this that after he already told us that our Patriarch Abraham, of blessed memory, did so, that he suffered it all for the sake of the Lord, then it is certain that everything that our Patriarch Abraham, peace be upon him, did was all according to accepted Torah law, so therefore why did Maimonides need to tell us that "it is the law that one must do so"? Do we dare imagine that our Patriarch Abraham, peace be upon him, did something, Heaven forbid, that was against Torah law? Thus we must say that it is possible to think that that which our Patriarch Abraham, peace be upon him, acted thusly, he did this out of an expression of extra piety, for a pious individual who is separated from the vanities of this world is permitted to sacrifice himself for the commandments even in a case where it is not obligatory to sacrifice one's soul, therefore Maimonides was careful to clearly state the detail that that which he did was according to the law, for the law is that one is required to do so for His Glory, therefore every person is required to do thus, and one should never think about what people will say, if it concerns an issue that is for the Glory of God, may His Name be blessed, and for the Glory of His Holy Torah.

There is what to analyze further within the above quoted words of Our Sages in Tractate Shabbos, that in Tractate Yevamoth p. 65b where it is taught that "just as it is a mitzvah to say that which will be heard, so is it a mitzvah to refrain from saying that which will not be heard. Rabbi Abba said it is an obligation to refrain, as it is said "do not rebuke a scoffer" (Proverbs 9:8). And

Rabbenu Bachaye in the beginning of his commentary on the book of Exodus writes that there are three groups that we are commanded not to rebuke, and they are scoffers, fools, and wicked people, and he brings proofs to all of this from Scripture. We must divide these in the way that *Tosafoth* does there in Tractate Shabbos, that where there is a doubt whether there might accept the rebuke, one must rebuke, as is mentioned there above, "who revealed this to them?"; however, if we know clearly that they will not accept the rebuke, we are not to rebuke them. And we need to understand, as there is apparently this question: how is it possible for a person to know for certain what will be after this, if the person will or will not accept the rebuke, for who revealed this to human beings? Thus, we need to say that this refers to the case where one can fairly presume that this person has established himself as one who will not accept rebuke, since we administer capital punishments such as stoning and burning based on well-established legal presumptions (*chazakah*), thus such a presumption can be considered as a certainty. Or, some say, according to that which the Holy Alshich wrote in his commentary on Proverbs, on the scripture "if sinners entice you, you should not consent..." (Proverbs 1:10), with his analysis of the passage, asking why was it necessary for the Scripture to warn us not to listen to those who entice us to spill innocent blood, and he explains that the intent in this is that when it comes to the one who says to spill innocent blood one should not consent to listen to him to join together with him for any reason, even for a good thing. And perhaps you might say that by staying away from the wicked you have nullified the commandment of causing the wicked to repent and return to God, to this he says that if one is so brazen {p. 13} faced to cause you to sin by murdering together with him, or similar sins without shame, then he will never be ashamed enough to receive any rebuke from you and to repent of his evil, therefore you should not consent to be with him in any endeavor, see there where he elaborates upon this teaching. We find that according to the words of the Alshich that one who is arrogant enough to publicly invite others to sin together with him, this is one who will certainly not receive rebuke.

And according to this there is what to understand why the Attribute of Strict Justice prosecuted against these righteous people and said "who revealed this to them?", for were they not already rebuked by Jeremiah and Ezekiel the prophets whose appointments were from the Mouth of the Lord, and all of this did not accomplish anything for them, therefore they were already established by force of legal presumption that they would not receive rebuke, which is considered as certain. It seems from this that only concerning an individual or a group where it is known that each and every individual is certainly established by force of legal presumption that they will not accept rebuke, then it is forbidden to rebuke them. However, when it concerns all of the general Israelite nation, either in its entirety or its majority, or even simply a large portion of the general nation of Israel, that it is impossible to know clearly if there will not be found among them those of the proper path who are suited to accept rebuke, and that occasionally the words will penetrate many of them and make an impression upon their hearts to turn them around to the good way, and therefore was it said "who revealed this to them?", as if to say that it was not revealed to them the levels that exist in all of the various souls there are among the Israelites, for perhaps a few people will be found for whom the rebuke will be valuable.

And it is possible for them to think that since, after all, most of the people can be categorized among those who it is legally presumed that they will not accept rebuke and it is thus forbidden to rebuke them, there is no further reason to suspect that there may be a minority who will accept in such a case, particularly where it is doubtful that such a minority even exists, whereas the status of the majority is a certainty that they will not accept rebuke and it is thus forbidden to rebuke them, thus one may think that in such a case we do not take consideration for a doubtful situation when one of certainty exists (Talmud: Avodah Zarah 41b, Niddah 15b, etc.). And it is possible that this is dependent upon that dispute in Tractate Yoma p. 84 if we take the majority into consideration when there is a case of danger to life, see there where the various sides of the dispute are discussed. Therefore, at a time when the Attribute of Mercy was ruling in the world, there was a measure of favorable judgement upon them, as it was said concerning them that they fulfilled the entire Torah from Aleph to Tav, however afterwards at the time when the Attribute of Strict Justice ruled there was prosecution against them, saying "who revealed this to them" that there would not be some effect by their rebuke to whatever small minority of people. In any event, they were punished so much with such a severe punishment, may the Merciful One save us, despite the fact that they were perfectly righteous and they fulfilled the entire Torah from Aleph until Tav, except for that one sin that they did not go to protest against the people of their generation to the point where they were endangered by violent physical retribution by the sinners. And also, during a time of mercy they only had the favorable judgement because it was indeed revealed and know before God that their rebuke would not be accepted, for the righteous were righteous without this, and all of those who were sunken into sin at that time did not have among them one who would receive rebuke, but who revealed this to them? This was still actually a doubt before them, therefore they were obligated to protest.

And consider this, the prohibition against rebuking those who will not accept rebuke does not apply to the masses, and we say clearly that the words of rebuke are only directed to those who will accept the rebuke, that is if there is found among them one who will accept rebuke, but not to those who are not receiving it, as I will bring later on clear words from the book "*Mayan Ganim*". And in our case, even though most of the world are caught in this net that was set by the heretical Zionists who cause the masses to sin, may the Merciful One save us, and to them there will be no effect even by words that are clearer than the noontime sun, for they will neither consent nor even consider to listen, and just the opposite they will add to their heresy, however against this it is clear without any doubt that there are still to be found among the Israelites some who follow the upright path who will accept words of rebuke into whom the word of truth will enter their hearts, and there will be value to them clear words that will enlighten their eyes. And even though they are a small minority, I have already written above that if even one Jew will be made to think after reading this it is extremely precious to illuminate his eyes and to stand him up upon the truth. And after investigating one can testify that there can still be found among the Israelites whole-hearted people who will come to understand, and therefore it is a tremendous obligation to clarify the revealed truth in the eyes of all, and we will still find hearts of good people both on the walls of the synagogues and study halls, as well as outside in the streets who will find some purpose from this. And this is especially so if it is a subject that touches upon all of the foundations of the Faith and the fulfillment of the entire Torah, for all of the deeds that are committed against the Holy Torah are a contradiction against the Faith, and all the more so that Zionist State which is entirely against the Holy Torah, and founded upon dreadful apostacy, may the Merciful One save us! For there is no doubt that it is entirely contrary to the Faith in the Blessed Lord and in His Holy Torah, and it is impossible to have these two faiths - the faith in this State, and the Faith in the Holy Torah - in one person, for they are two total opposites, and it is impossible for them both to operate with a single crown, as will be further explained in the continuation of this pamphlet inside. And even among those who lack understanding, who do not feel this at the outset, in the end they will come to understand, as the *Akeidah* writes in his commentary to Parshas V'Es'chanan (Deuteronomy 3-7) concerning those who worship a partnership of deity (i.e. another deity partnering with the True God), that in the end they will entirely abandon the Blessed Lord and will remain simply with their foreign idolatry, see there as he elaborates in his words, and this is also so with all of those who "hold between two opinions" (I Kings 18:21).

{p. 14}

And in Jeremiah 14 verse 13(-16): "Then I said: 'Ah, Lord GOD! behold, the prophets say unto them: You shall not see the sword, neither shall you have famine; but I will give you assured peace in this place.' Then the LORD said to me: 'The prophets prophesy lies in My name; I sent them not, neither have I commanded them, [neither spoke I unto them;] they prophesy unto you a lying vision, and divination, and a thing of nought, and the deceit of their own heart. Therefore, thus says the LORD: As for the prophets [that prophesy in My name, and I sent them not, yet they say: Sword and famine shall not be in this land, by sword and famine shall those prophets be consumed;] and the people to whom they prophesy [shall be cast out in the streets of Jerusalem because of the famine and the sword;]" etc. - And consider this that is self-evident that it is impossible to explain this passage by saying that the prophet Jeremiah was telling over to God what the false prophets were saying as a reproof and complaint, for was it not known that they had no truth in them, rather Rabbi David Kimchi and the other commentators explain that this is a prayer and an expression of favorable judgement upon Israel, and this is how the *Targum Jonathan* translates, that "Jeremiah said, 'accept my prayer, Oh Lord,'", for since the false prophets were causing them to stumble in folly, therefore they were not guilty and it was not proper to punish them, for what can be done to the people who do not know how to discern between the Truth and falsehood, and through this did he wish to save them from the punishment that God warned them of. And according to this there is what to understand in what God answered them that they were false prophets, for did Jeremiah not already know this, but rather His intention was to extend some favorable judgement to the Israelites, and from the Blessed Creator's answer in the verse it seems that there really is no answer to his words as it is known that there is no favorable judgement in Jeremiah's words. However, the *RaDa"K* elaborates upon his explanation there, that those false prophets did have the power to tell the future and it was clarified inasmuch as they were justified in their words concerning many subjects, therefore it was possible to fool the Israelites that they should not be afraid of Jeremiah's words that warn them of the punishments, for they calmed their minds by saying that they see through prophecy that there will not be any sword or famine and they were making their evil deeds seem nice. This is what God said, despite the fact that the false prophets are fooling them, in any event it was their responsibility to discern the difference between the true prophets and the false prophets. For a true prophet will stand them up upon the Torah of Moses, whereas the false prophets will make idolatry seem attractive to them, as this is the nullification of Torah study, and even though they were made aware that some of the future predictions made by the false prophets were fulfilled, with all of that they should have said that they could tell the future through sorcery rather than prophecy, for do not their words lead to the nullification of the Torah, which is like idolatry, for even if they perform signs and wonders the Torah says they should be put to death if their words are rotten (Deuteronomy 13). And the Scripture already explains the reason why those signs and wonders of false prophets and sorcerers may be fulfilled, for "the LORD your God is testing you" (Deuteronomy 13:4), these are a summary of his words, see there in the commentary of Rabbi

David Kimchi.

It is clearly explained from all of this that everything that is sourced from these who uproot our religion, may the Merciful One save us, that it is clear that this is not from the side of the Blessed Lord, but rather that God allows them to perform these things in order to test the Jews, therefore as it was in the days of Jeremiah, when the First Temple was destroyed, that the Children of Israel were punished with such a bitter punishment, that even though the false prophets were predicting the future and their words were being fulfilled, and even if there was no way to discern that their words were not true except through this test to see if their words were nullifying words of Torah, for this is certainly something which cannot be from the Lord, and even the prayer of the prophet

Jeremiah did not effect to have them judged favorably for they were fooled after the prophecies of the false prophets, for there is no place for doubt in the matter. In any event, with the establishment of that Zionist State, which has caused millions of Jews to leave our Faith, may the Merciful One save us, for this is clear that anyone who believes in the Blessed Lord will not have any doubt that they (Zionists) are the accursed source of defilement of heresy and apostacy, may the Merciful One save us, woe to us that this has arisen in our days. And how is it possible to be silent and see the uprooting of the fundamentals of the Faith and the foundations of the entire Torah?! Especially if all of the pious ones who are still to be found in our generation will place their hands on their mouths in order that they do not speak the truth, they have also hidden their hand from the printing plate that they do not write the truth out of fear of the generation; if so, the way of truth may be completely forgotten from the generation, Heaven forbid; and all that the Holy Geonim, their souls are in Eden, stormed the world in the previous generations, teaching us about the dangers of the Zionists who are destroying the world, all of this has practically been forgotten. And if also from now on our words be hidden and will not be revealed in the eyes of the world, if so then the truth of the fundamentals of the Faith and the foundations of the Holy Torah will be totally forgotten, Heaven forbid, that even if the Blessed Lord helps us that there will still come a time when the storm of the Zionists will be silenced, but since the path of Truth would be forgotten and there would be no person to set on their heart who would teach knowledge and who would understand a teaching to restore the elevated status of Torah, for the silence of the entire generation could certainly be considered totally as the saying goes "silence is admittance" (Talmud Kerithoth 11b, etc.), and it would never again arise upon the heart to contemplate how far the world has been immersed and drowned in this tremendous falsehood that destroys the entire Torah. And therefore there is a great and tremendous responsibility upon us to cry out like an announcer to reveal to all Israel the word against the deep impurity that has spread so much in our generation, and our hope is that we will find many people even if it does not effect them at all now, in any event not all times are equal, and there will still come a time that some of the hearts of the Children of Israel will be open and their eyes will open and the voices sounding from the ancient paths will reach their ears, that they will seek Truth and proper Faith. However, this will not be so if the voices are quieted, Heaven forbid, and "there is no speech, there are no words, neither is their voice heard" (Psalm 19:4) in all of the borders of Israel, Heaven forbid, {p. 15} and all hope would be lost. I have already brought from the words of Maimonides that according to the law each and every one is obligated to suffer it all from the people of the generation for the sake of the Glory of the Blessed Lord and His Holy Torah, just as our Patriarch Abraham, peace be upon him, suffered.

And furthermore, there in Jeremiah 5 in the verse, "Run to and fro through the streets of Jerusalem, and see now, and know, and seek in the broad places thereof, if you can find a man, if there be any that does justly, that seeks truth; and I will pardon her." (Jeremiah 5:1) All of the commentators are amazed by this, for do we not find that there were then many righteous and holy people, and how could it be said that no man was found? And the RaDa"K comments there in the name of his father of blessed memory that Jeremiah said this in the open streets of Jerusalem, as he said "and seek in the broad places thereof", for the pious people that were in Jerusalem locked themselves in their houses and were not able to show themselves publicly in the streets and broad places, because of the wicked people. Similarly, the Holy ShLa"H explained that that is the reason the verse refers to the "streets" and "broad places", for if they were not afraid of the people to reveal the truth in the streets and wide places they would be protected. And the RAV"A writes in his commentary to Parshas Vayera on the verse "And the LORD said: 'If I find in Sodom fifty righteous within the city, then I will forgive all the place for their sake.'" (Genesis 18:26), and these are his words: "and the reason it says 'within the city', is to teach that they would be those who fear the Lord publicly, similarly 'Run to and fro through the streets of Jerusalem' (Jeremiah 5:1)" until here are his words. And it is explained by this that this is also the explanation behind the Scripture "Run to and fro through the streets of Jerusalem", that the intent is that they should do so publicly, letting piety be known in the "streets" and "wide places". And this also explains the intent behind the prayer of our Patriarch Abraham, peace be upon him, that he said "within the city", meaning that they fear the Lord publicly, that they are not afraid of the people of the city. And from these words we can ask, why our Patriarch Abraham, peace be upon him, did not begin to pray for righteous people like these who are afraid to tell the truth in the midst of the city, for even righteous people like these have the power to protect the city. One must say from this that one knows that it is certain that righteous people like this are not able to protect the city, and therefore he did not pray concerning this. And this is clear that in Sodom it was certainly a great and difficult test of character to reveal one's opinion of pious fear of the Lord publicly in the midst of the city, for anyone who went on the path of truth took his life in his hands, as is known from the story that there was one person who was killed for giving bread to a poor person, and what is openly explained in Scripture that they surrounded Lot's house because he fulfilled the mitzvah of hospitality, and he brought the angels into his house, and if this is so there was a clear and strong legal presumption that they would not receive rebuke, and despite this he only prayed for those righteous people who were not afraid of the people of the city.

It is clear that Maimonides wrote in the *Hilchoth Deoth* (The Laws of Temperaments) Chapter 6, that from a country where people do not follow the proper path one should escape from there even to caves, forests, and deserts, and in the Talmud Avodah Zara p. 18 it is expounded concerning Abraham, "Happy is the man that does not walk in the advice of the wicked" (Psalm 1:1), this is Abraham who did not follow the advice of the generation of the dispersion (the Tower of Babel), "and in the path of sinners he did not stand" (ibid.), that he did not stand in the group of the Sodomites, "for the men of Sodom were sinners" (Genesis 13:13). It seems that we cannot understand why Abraham would be praised for not following in the path of such totally wicked sinners as these and following their advice, for was he not the choicest creation on earth in his day, even compared to the other righteous people, and not only when compared to totally wicked people like these, and the Holy Torah also holds Lot guilty for failing to hold himself back from living in the same community as the people of Sodom, as Rashi says in his comments Parshas Lech Lecha in verse 13 (Genesis 13:13), and this is not considered to be a praise to Abraham. Rather, therefore the intent is that he did not stand with them even with good intentions in order to make spiritual rectifications among them, for when a righteous person stands between wicked people like this it damages the world for they are drawn after them. And the MaHaRSh"A, of blessed memory, writes there that he did not stand with the people of Sodom even in a place where it was proper to stand with them, meaning to stand with them in the war that the people of Sodom had against the four kings (Genesis 14) in order to save Lot he did not stand with them, and therefore they fell in the war until Abraham needed afterward to pursue after the four kings to save Lot. And in another place, I elaborated upon an explanation of what it was said that he did not follow the advice of the generation of the dispersion after the Tower of Babel, and this is not its place. However, in any event, this is certain, that one needs to run away from joining together with the wicked in order not to learn from their deeds, but one should not hold back from publicizing the words that teach the path of fear of the Lord even in the "midst of the city", "in the streets" and "in her open places".

And the ChaSa"M Sofer, of blessed memory, writes in Parshas Ki Sisa on the Scripture "And he said to Moses there is the sound of war in the camp" (Exodus 32:17), meaning that Joshua also understood that it was a voice of shouting, but he thought that logic dictates that it is impossible that the righteous people would be quiet when this deed was done, and thus he assumed there was a "war in the camp", and Moses also thought this as well, for that was the reason why he brought the Tablets and did not leave them in heaven nor break them in heaven, for he thought there were righteous people among them, but when he arrived and sensed that there was no war here, etc., and therefore it was proper to immediately break the tablets, but we do not pass judgement based on circumstantial evidence, until he saw it himself, etc." Until here are his words. And this is the logical assumption that our teacher Moses, peace be upon him, was forced to take, for if this was done in the generation an abomination like this it is impossible to let it pass in silence, that no war would be waged against it whatsoever in any event that some sound of war would be heard in the camp. And all the more so this evil abomination of the Zionist State which violates the serious oaths that God made us swear {p. 16}, and also that it violates our religion and roots heresy and apostacy into the entire world, and it prevents our salvation and the redemption of our souls, for certainly one must wage war against this impure idea with self-sacrifice until the point where the Lord will look down from Heaven and see us, and have mercy upon us to take us out from this bitter and painful Exile and open the eyes of Israel to see the Truth and to return to the Blessed Lord and to His Holy Torah.

And I saw fit to copy here the words of the Holy Master, our teacher, the Rebbe Tzvi Elimelech Shapira of Dinov, of blessed memory, author of the book "Bnei Yissaschar", who wrote in his introduction to the book "Mayan Ganim" with tremendous enthusiasm and with abundant zealotry against those who seek to uproot our religion in Israel, and he writes at the end of his words, and it is thus quoted: "And this is to make it know, my dear reader, that my intent in my words to fight against the free-spirited wicked heretics, is only that they should know the Truth and return to the Lord. For the wise King Solomon already said 'A fool does not desire understanding' (Proverbs 18:2), and 'one should know what to answer a heretic' (Avoth 2:19) which Rabbi Yochanan taught only refers to a gentile heretic, but to a Jewish heretic all the more so as he will make his heresy stronger (Talmud Sanhedrin 38b), and he said all the more so that by a Jewish heretic it is forbidden to answer him, since he does not want an answer but rather he wants to reveal his heart with further heresy in order to remove from him the burden of the Torah and divine Service, and even if you answer him with bundles and bundles of answers, he will work hard and strengthen himself to repeat his twisted folly to answer more against your words, and each time he will be encourages to follow more unrestrained words by further expounding upon his words with him with various arguments. And this is what Rashi, of blessed memory, wanted to say, that if you answer him he will be extremely deliberate to answer your words with false responses and various sayings and insulting jokes, etc., therefore Heaven forbid I should fail to follow the path brought by our ancestors, violating the words of our Sages, of blessed memory. But my will in my words is only to argue with the wicked in order to stand them on the truth. I know, I know, that if they see these words of mine that are said in truth they will go on to expand their heresy by answering with sayings and insulting jokes, for this is their path all day, "and foreign lips are sweet" (Proverbs 5:3). However, my entire desire in these words of mine is to save the confused souls of our brothers the Children of Israel, to save the young children who have no blemish and to warn them to stay far away from wandering toward the tents of these wicked men who have thrown off the yoke of the burden of the words of our Sages from their necks and have even spoken ill against the commandments of the Lord that are clearly written Biblically in the Written Torah, for they are even worse than the Karaite sect who have already been pushed away from the Children of Israel from taking hold of the string of the Heritage of the Lord until they have turned to become a distinct people to themselves like the other gentile nations. And behold these people are even worse than them, as they are mixed from the Mixed Multitude from the Amalekites, etc. Our brethren, the Children of Israel, please distance yourselves from the tents of these wicked men and do not join with them in any way... etc." See there as he elaborates upon his holy words with flames of fire.

I copied here a portion of his holy quotations, for through this we can learn much about our present era, for the wicked people in our generation are millions of levels worse than the wicked people of his generation, and one can contemplate upon this how much one needs to stay far away from them. Also, he clearly stated that he was not speaking to the heretics concerning which our Sages forbade us to answer, and by saying this he fulfilled his obligation to refrain from violating the words of Our Sages. Similarly I am saying the same, that I am not writing at all to any of those sects that our Sages have forbade us to rebuke, but rather to that minority of people who are seeking to know the truth, and only from the influence of the majority of the world with all of their various parties and groups who are drawn after the Zionists who confuse the minds, and from them it is possible to still save precious souls. Also, there are many who are bribed whether it be with honor or money, or because they are afraid of their congregations and the like, and all of these are unable to admit to the truth, for it has been hidden from them, for the Holy Torah says that "the bribe blinds the eyes of the wise" (Exodus 23:8, Deuteronomy 16:19), and our Sages elaborate upon this in Tractate Kesubos p. 105 as to how much one's eyes can be blinded even by verbal bribery, and all the more so with a substantial bribery, and one who is blind and his vision is impaired cannot even see the noontime sun, so how could he see the truth? But with all of this there are still found in Israel people whose hearts have not been bribed so much that they do not recognize the truth.

I know that the teachers will shoot arrows and spears without measure against the words that I have written, for this has been the path of the Zionists forever, and all the more so the religious people who have been drawn after them, to pour out insult and mockery, scorn and scoffing, and enormous and awesome lies and falsehoods against anyone who is not drawn after their opinions and does not follow in their footsteps, and they reveal facets of Torah which violate the true path of Torah law with their many vanities in an immeasurable proportion, for there is no end to empty words filled with hot air, however I bless the Lord who has guided me in the advice not to think at all of their vain and empty words which have no value. And I hope to the Blessed Lord who helps and supports to illuminate the eyes of those who are waiting patiently for Him to see the Truth, and may the Blessed Lord make us worthy that the Name of Heaven should be sanctified by our hands until we be worthy to the complete Redemption and "the Earth will be filled with knowledge of the Lord" (Isaiah 11:9), soon and in our days, Amen.

{p. 17}

And we see in the lengthy commentary of the RaDa"K on the Psalms that in many of the Psalms he comes to contradict the opinions of the

Christians who try to bring proofs from those Psalms to the person from Nazereth, may the Merciful One save us. Also, Maimonides in the "Epistle to Yemen" writes to contradict that which one person attempted to bring proofs from the Holy Torah for Mohammed. And behold, the Christians come with many lengthy works of apologetic literature with various proofs, and the RaDa"K does not bring them all, for it is impossible to deal with all of the lies and imaginations that have no measure, despite that the RaDa"K toiled in many Psalms to explain so there would be no place to make a mistake, Heaven forbid, according to the opinions of the Christians, and those who seek the truth come to realizations even to the other words that were not brought in the words of the RaDa"K, and the Truth testifies for itself. And in these generations of ours, that is what the religious people who are dragged after the Zionists and partnering with them, for they bring proofs from the Holy Torah to support the opinions of Zionism, with various garbs, and through this they cause even the hearts of those who follow the upright path to be drawn to folly, just as the Sadducees, the Nazarenes, and the Sabatteans, and all of those who seek to uproot the Holy Torah have done in their times. And furthermore, from this today we see that this has been clothed in a Jerusalemite Garb, in the name of love of the Land and salvation of Israel, and these lies and outrageous mockeries are so abundant without measure in order to fool the eyes of people.

And in this pamphlet, I have incidentally written in order to contradict some of the concepts that have spread from them to the world in order to fool people, and anyone who had a brain in his skull will see the truth, but it is impossible to deal with all of their vanities, falsehoods, empty fantasies, and words of mockery to bring answers to all of them in writing, for there is no end to words filled with hot air, and garments of falsehood, and their dishonest fantasies for they have no end, but if one will set his heart to the Word of the Lord he will see that all of their words are vanities of vanity, which have no substance, and the wind can carry them all away. And now, in the footsteps of the Messianic Era, before the final separation of good and evil, the Other Side of Evil has strengthened itself with the power of the enticers and tempters through these religious people who are dragged after the Zionists more than it strengthened itself with all of the enticers and tempters throughout all of the generations who were from the day the world was created until today, and all of the smoothing of the tongue of the Original Serpent that was by Adam the First Man, and also all of the smooth talk of all of the tempters and enticers that were throughout all of the generations in various garbs, all of them together do not reach at all to that measure of smooth talk of the tempters and enticers of our times, who use various and varied techniques to go down to the inner chambers of the belly of every Jew, for that is how it is before the nullification of the Other Side of Evil from Israel, as I have brought above from the *Tosfos Yom Tov*, and we need tremendous mercy to be rescued from them and their masses. May the Blessed Lord have mercy upon us with His Tremendous Mercy without any measure or limit, and may He speedily "cause us to rejoice according to number of the days of our affliction" (Psalm 90:15), and may we be worthy to come close to Him, may His Name be blessed, with holiness and purity, and to soon see the salvation of all Israel and in their joy, soon and in our days, Amen.

* * *

And I called the name of this pamphlet "*VaYoel Moshe*" (Exodus 2:21), for two reasons. The first reason is because Our Sages said in Sifri on Deuteronomy, and in many places in Midrashim, and it is also so in the Talmud Tractate Nedarim p. 65a, that the word "*VaYoel*" means only a term of swearing to an oath, as it says "*VaYoel Shaul*, and Saul swore to the people" (I Samuel 14:24).

Since the purpose of this pamphlet is to explain the oath that God made Israel swear (to wait for the Messiah), therefore it was fitting to entitle it by the name "*VaYoel Moshe*". And even though this Oath is found in the Song of Songs, in any event it is explained in Midrash Rabba, Parshas Yisro, chapter 28, that everything that the Prophets were destined to prophesy in the future in every generation was already received at Mount Sinai, as Moses said to them to Israel "but with him that stands here with us this day before the LORD our God, and also with him that is not here with us this day" (Deuteronomy 29:14). And this is particularly so with the Song of Songs, for the Rabbis have said clearly that it was from Sinai, as was brought by the Alshich, of blessed memory, and all which was given at Sinai was by our Teacher Moses, peace be upon him, therefore this oath can also be termed with the saying "*VaYoel Moshe*" - "And Moses swore", that he caused Israel to swear, just like it is written "*VaYoel Shaul*", that Saul caused the people to swear, by taking an oath. And also what our Sages expounded there in its place that Jethro caused Moses to take an oath that he would not return to Egypt without his permission, which was also similar to this Oath, for it would seem that this would not be understood, since Jethro saw that our Teacher Moses, peace be upon him, was a holy man, for it is explained in the Midrash Rabba there that he saw that the water was blessed on his account, and other miracles, and it is explained in Pirkei D'Rabbi Eliezer, chapter 40, that the Staff that was created during the twilight of the Sixth Day of Creation was given to Adam the first man in the Garden of Eden, and later to the holy

Patriarchs, until it came to Egypt, and Jethro took it and planted it in the garden of his house, and no man was able to come close to it again, and when Moses came to his house, he went to the garden of Jethro's house and he saw the Staff and read the initial letters that were on it, and he sent forth his hand and took it. When Jethro saw this, he said that this man is destined to redeem the Israelites from Egypt, therefore he gave his daughter Zipporah to him as his wife, see there. If this is so, did not Jethro see that Moses was the redeemer of Israel, and it was certain that he would not be suspected of falsehood nor of failing to stand by his word, if that is so why did he have to make him swear? Is it not enough that he would promise? Why specifically should it be through an oath? Perhaps the answer is that Jethro knew that Moses was destined to return to Egypt to redeem

Israel, and thus the redemption was dependent upon him, and from this they both feared lest perhaps due to his abundant {p. 18} love for his fellow Israelites, when he saw the affliction of his people and their tremendous pain that they suffered with the yoke of the Exile, perhaps he would go early there before the proper time, therefore he made him swear. And we also see that our Patriarch Abraham, peace be upon him, perform various gestures to ensure that David the son of Jesse would not come before the proper time, as Our Sages expound upon the verse "And Abram sent them back" (Genesis 15:11). Therefore, it is ideal to connect an oath to this concept, for one will certainly not violate an oath, and thereby come to push the end-times. And this oath was also similar to those that God caused us to swear. And so it was, that also after that, when

God sent him to redeem Israel, he needed to return to Midian to be released from his oath in Jethro's presence, as is explained in the Talmud, Tractate Nedarim p. 65. And that which Moses tried to deny his appointment was also known to be for the good of Israel, for he saw that the time was not yet fulfilled and they would need to complete it with other Exiles, therefore he wished to delay the redemption on the only condition that his redemption would be the Complete Redemption after which no other Exile would follow. However, the time was not yet ripe for this then, for they were not able to wait as Scripture attests, and as the Ariza"l explains as is known (that they would descend into the fiftieth gate of impurity and not be able to be redeemed). And in *Yismach Moshe* from my holy grandfather, of blessed and sacred memory, in Parshas Shemini he writes that Moses' intention in attempting to deny his appointment was in order that the redemption would be by God Himself in His full Glory, see there. In any event, this Oath is also able to be termed with the words "*VaYoel Moshe*", for all came through our Teacher Moses, peace be upon him. And the Targum in Song of Songs on the verse "I cause you to swear, oh daughters of Jerusalem" (Song of Songs 2:7, 3:5, 8:4) etc. opening: "after this was said to Moses in a prophecy", and it is clear from this that the Oaths came through our Teacher Moses, peace be upon him. However the Targum writes this concerning the first oaths that according to his opinion concerned the Generation of the Wilderness that were in the days of our Teacher Moses, peace be upon him, but the later Oath the Targum writes there is said concerning the King Messiah, for the

King Messiah is under an Oath not to push us out of the Exile until the Will comes from before the Lord of the Universe, as we see according to his opinion the last Oath applies to our generation, for it comes from the King Messiah, but according to that which is explained in the Holy Zohar and in many Midrashim that the King Messiah is actually our Teacher Moses, peace be upon him, and what is explained in many places that the King Messiah is David, the Holy Or HaChaim already answered this in Parshas Vayechi on the Scripture "Tying his foal to a vine" (Genesis 49:11), that the King Messiah will include them both, if so this Oath is also included in the terminology "*VaYoel Moshe*". And especially according to that which I have written that without this the revelation of the prophecy concerning these Oaths was from Sinai, and all that was said at Sinai was through the hand of our Teacher Moses, peace be upon him, so therefore it is certainly worthwhile to attach this term of "*VaYoel Moshe*" to these Oaths.

And the second reason is, that in this title there is mention of my poor name together with the holy name of my holy grandfather the Yismach Moshe, of blessed and sacred memory, who sacrificed his soul all of his life for the Redemption, and he said that for this reason he sacrificed his soul for the Redemption more than the other saintly *Tzadikim*, because hearing of a thing does not compare to seeing it, and everyone heard about the destruction of the Temple, but he, of blessed memory, saw it with his own eyes, for he was in that generation (in a previous incarnation), and everything that happened then stands before his eyes, and there is no doubt that even now he is standing and begging for mercy upon Israel and upon the Holiness of God's Blessed Name, as he promised, and this violation of the oaths is the thing that is preventing the Redemption and is bringing all of the suffering, Heaven forbid. May the merit of my holy ancestor, of blessed and sacred memory, together with all of the righteous and holy people, protect us to be saved from this trouble. May the Blessed Lord have mercy upon His people Israel in all the places that they dwell, and say to our troubles that it is enough, and may we not have any more pain, and may our supplications be close to the Lord our God day and night, to turn our hearts to Him to walk in all of His ways and to return to Him, may His Name be Blessed, with satisfaction and joy without trouble or injury, and may the Glory of the Holy Torah and of Israel be raised soon, and among the general people of Israel may the Blessed Lord also have mercy upon me, the lowly and poor one, for my heart is broken within me and I stand and I wait only for Heavenly Mercy. May the merit of my holy ancestors protect me to merit salvation and mercy, and may we be worthy again to do perfect repentance and to serve the Blessed Lord with a good heart as is His Will, may His Name be blessed, until we are worthy to see soon the salvation of all Israel and their joy, soon and in our days, Amen!

Printed in Great Britain
by Amazon